TWO UP
and a bag of chips!

- - - - - - - - -

GEORGE'S CONEY ISLAND:
SERVING THE WORCESTER COMMUNITY
FOR OVER 100 YEARS

KATHRYN TSANDIKOS

with Holly Robinson

TIDEPOOL PRESS
Cambridge, Massachusetts

Copyright © 2021 by Kathryn Tsandikos
Published in the United States in 2021 by TidePool Press

TidePool Press
6 Maple Avenue, Cambridge, Massachusetts 02139
www.tidepoolpress.com

Printed in the United States

Library of Congress Cataloging-in-Publication Data

Tsandikos, Kathryn 1958–
	Two Up and a Bag of Chips: George's Coney Island, Serving the Worcester
	Community for Over 100 Years

	ISBN 978-0-9978482-9-8
	1. Tsandikos, Kathryn—History
	2. Food—Worcester, Massachusetts 3. Greek culture
	4. Entrepreneurship 5. Immigration—United States
	I. Title.

	2021903052

PHOTO AND ART CREDITS: COVERS AND PP. 1–6
Front cover: George's Coney Island at night. Photo by Michael J. West.
Page 1: Entrance to George's Coney Island, 2020. Photo by Mike Henderickson.
Page 2: Two "Up" and a Bag of Chips. Painting by Mark Waitkus.
Page 6: Worcester Collage. Illustration by Faye Guanipa, Olive & Company.
Back cover: George Tsagarelis, from the Tsandikos family archives.

*This book is dedicated to my family and to all of the
George's Coney Island lovers, young and old. Your patronage, loyalty,
and fierce passion have kept our doors open for more than 100 years.*

*This book is also dedicated to Worcester and its people.
It is an honor to be a part of this great city's history.*

Faye Guanipa is a New England-based illustrator and surface pattern designer. She is a proud Worcester resident and works closely with several local small businesses representing their brands through illustration and design. She also owns a small stationery company, Olive & Company, selling paper goods and greeting cards locally and throughout the nation. Follow her journey on Instagram @oliveandcopaper and @faye_guanipa.illustration.

CONTENTS

. . . .

Part 5 CONEY ISLAND INSPIRATION 109

Part 6 A LOOK TO THE FUTURE 135

Kathy Tsandikos and her father, Fr. Solon Tsandikos, enjoying time together, c. 2018.
Fr. Tsandikos passed away in fall of 2020. He is missed.
Courtesy of the *Worcester Telegram & Gazette*

Introduction

When I was a young boy, I used to come to Coney Island after the Boys Club. I had a dime to spend—a nickel on a hot dog and a nickel on a chocolate milk. Today is my dad's birthday. He could have had any meal and gone to any restaurant, but he always wanted to come to Coney Island. Today is the anniversary of his death, and we came here to celebrate his memory. My name is carved in one of those booths over there.

—A CONEY ISLAND FAN

I feel so lucky. Nearly every day, I hear stories like this from our customers at Coney Island. They remind me that our family restaurant has become much more than just a great place to grab a quick hot dog. Through the last century, Coney Island has become a touchstone for generations of families making memories.

When my grandfather, a young Greek immigrant, first purchased George's Coney Island, I'm sure he never dreamed of the many changes the city of Worcester would undergo, or imagined that our small family business would outlast them all and grow into an iconic city landmark.

As I began thinking about creating a book to honor my family, Worcester, and Coney Island's 100th anniversary, my initial thought was to write a history of the restaurant paralleled with the city of Worcester, which has been built—and is still being developed—largely by people from many different countries who came with the singular, passionate goal of building a better life for themselves and their families. My grandfather George, who arrived from Greece as a boy of 16, was an entrepreneur who refused to give up no matter how many challenges he faced. Worcester's history is equally inspiring. From manufacturing to high tech, from its Depression-era struggle to its current incarnation as a dynamic 21st-century college and health care hub, the city has undergone many transformations.

Yet, despite the upheavals around us over the last century, much about our restaurant has remained the same. Coney Island has always been an oasis of sorts, drawing people from all walks of life and through every phase of Worcester's history. Today, we still serve hot dogs with our signature special sauce, and the Coney Island sign is as much of a landmark for Worcester as the Citgo sign is for Boston. Except for a few necessary updates, the restaurant even looks the same, right down to the wooden booths carved by thousands of lovers, soldiers, children, workers, bosses, and college students.

As I began writing this book, however, I quickly realized that I would be leaving out the very heart and soul of Coney Island if I didn't include at least some of the stories told by the thousands of people who have stepped through our doors. As I'm reminded every time I see someone take a selfie or post a picture of their lunch on Instagram, Coney Island is not only a historic restaurant where older customers can come to relive their childhoods. This is also a place where fresh memories are being made every day by new generations.

Maybe your own grandparents had their first date at Coney Island. Or maybe you came here every Saturday with your parents, and now you bring your kids to see us. Whatever your Coney Island traditions are, I hope you'll be reminded of them when you read this book, because most of all, I wrote this book to celebrate all of you—our loyal customers. We're honored to be even a small part of your family traditions. We love you and don't take any of you for granted, and we're thrilled that you shared so many of your stories and photos with us for this book.

Our legacy is your legacy. In these pages, you'll read about everything from my grandfather's difficult ship passage from Greece to how we got our iconic sign, from the origin of our special sauce to the carvings on our wooden booths, from Worcester's manufacturing history to the current revitalization of downtown.

Woven throughout the book are your personal stories too, because *you* are the reason Coney Island has celebrated 100 years in business and is still going strong. I am overwhelmed with gratitude each time you share a Coney Island experience. We value them all. We are blessed to have had the opportunity to feed, listen to, care for, cry, and laugh with you.

Whether you've just discovered Coney Island or you're one of our regulars, this book is for you. If you have never been to Coney Island, we hope you will enjoy this story and come experience a taste of Worcester, Massachusetts, for yourself. May we have a hundred more years of memories to come. For as long as you let us, we will be here for you.

KATHRYN TSANDIKOS
Worcester, Massachusetts
November 11, 2020

• • • • • • • • • • • • • • • • •

(Opposite page) George's Coney Island exterior
Painting by Mark Waitkus

George's Coney Island has long been a favorite subject for the media. *Zippy the Pinhead* by Bill Griffith and articles, courtesy of the *Worcester Telegram & Gazette*, "2001 Book of Lists" cover, courtesy of *Worcester Business Journal*

George Tsagarelis at
George's Coney Island, c. 1950.

Part 1

GEORGE'S CONEY ISLAND

Sixty years ago, I had my first Coney Island hot dog … mustard and onions. Being a salesman in Worcester County, on the road all day, allowed me the opportunity to have this treat whenever I was in the area. Regardless of the time of day, I remember Coney Island always being busy, filled with people of all ages, from all walks of life, having one thing in common, the love of this unique hot dog. I also remember the unchanged décor and a rather unique toilet paper in the men's room! Oh, how I marveled at the man behind the counter who would stack hot dogs from the tip of his finger, up the length of his arm. The two gray-haired gentlemen always served with a smile. This week, my daughter and I stopped in for a hot dog treat. Sharing the experience, she now understands! I will soon be 90 years old. My memory of Coney Island hot dogs is one of my fondest of living in Worcester.

—Eliot Beren

Eliot passed away in 2018. His obituary in the *Worcester Telegram & Gazette* read: "Eliot always enjoyed a Coney Island hot dog, a trip to Spag's, Green Hill Park, and watching the boats on Lake Quinsigamond …"

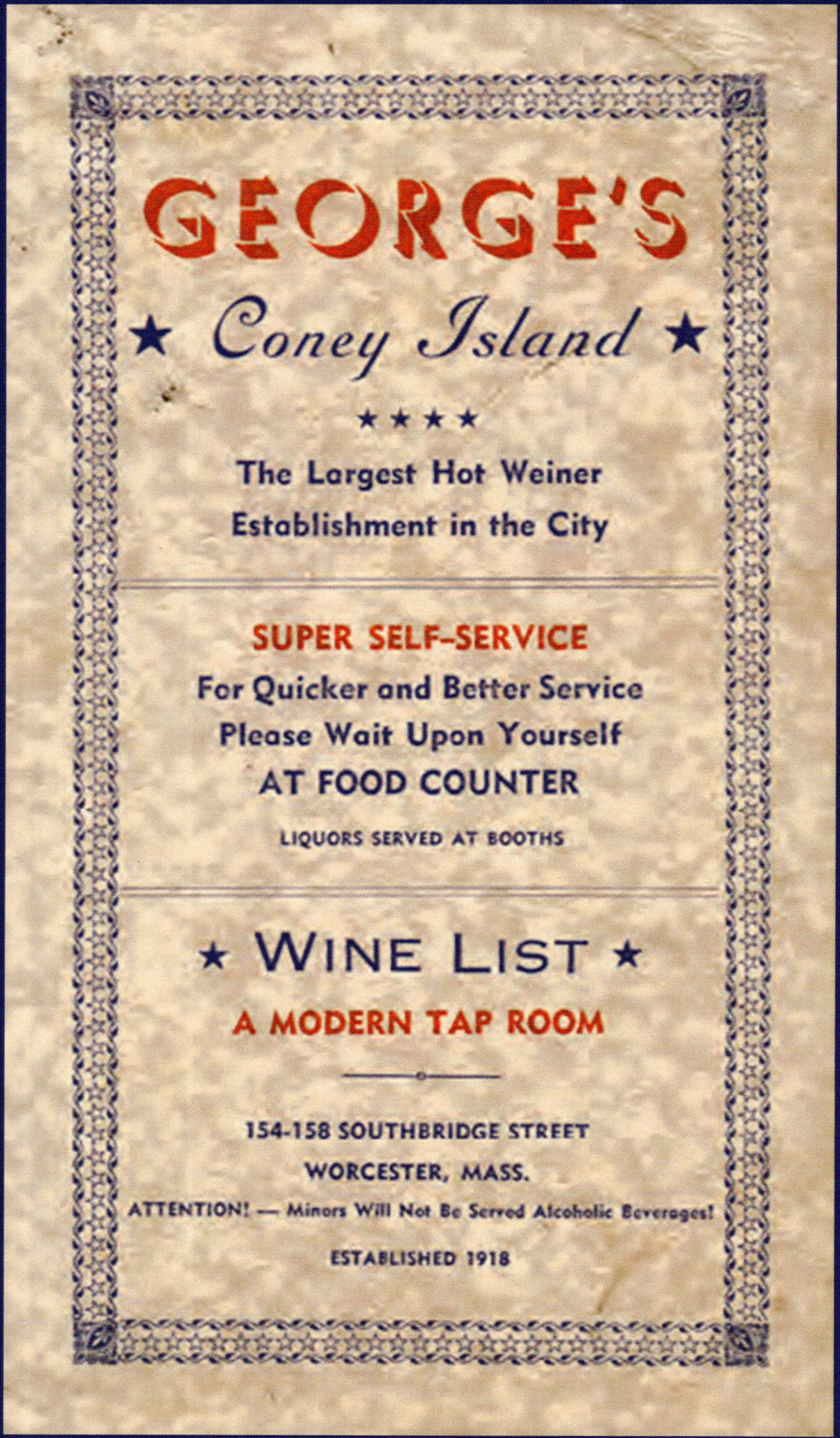

GEORGE'S

★ *Coney Island* ★

★★★★

The Largest Hot Weiner
Establishment in the City

SUPER SELF-SERVICE
For Quicker and Better Service
Please Wait Upon Yourself
AT FOOD COUNTER

LIQUORS SERVED AT BOOTHS

★ WINE LIST ★

A MODERN TAP ROOM

——○——

154-158 SOUTHBRIDGE STREET
WORCESTER, MASS.

ATTENTION! — Minors Will Not Be Served Alcoholic Beverages!

ESTABLISHED 1918

George Tsagarelis, c. 1940.

I would like to share my memories of Coney Island. I'm 73 ½ years old and was first brought there in 1947 with my grandfather. In my teens I went there with all my friends and carved my name in the walls. I remember watching the old man behind the counter with that wooden thing on his arm loading up the buns with that great sauce. I think they were eight for $1 then. As I said, I'm 73 ½ years old and they don't taste any different now. I come in twice a week and get three "up." Don't tell my doctor! Thanks for still being there for us.

—RAY LaMONDA

THE MAN WHO MADE CONEY ISLAND

My grandfather, George Tsagarelis, was a thickly-built man with large hands, a powerful personality, and a desire to have everything done just right. For the customers who still remember him, often their stories begin with something like this: "I remember George standing at the end of the counter and cutting the hot dogs," because, until the 1960s, when the hot dogs came in links, that's what George had to do. I don't even try to imagine how many hot dogs he must have cut up during his lifetime.

What I do imagine is how hard he worked. When he first closed down the original luncheonette and opened Coney Island in its current location in 1926, George came in early and stayed until two or three o'clock in the morning.

Growing up, I heard stories of my grandfather hopping over the counter and chasing men down the street if he thought they were out of line. For instance, George couldn't stand seeing people sitting in the booths of his restaurant and putting their feet up on the booth opposite, either. He wouldn't ask them to put their feet down. He'd just walk by and knock their feet right off the booth. George was a tough guy and fiercely protective of his business.

But I knew another side of my grandfather, too—a soft, generous, and loving side. He loved to tell me stories of how hard he tried to fit in as an immigrant, calling himself a "greenhorn." Many of those stories were about surviving unimaginable hardships. Unimaginable, and yet common for immigrants like George who, in his early days as a businessman, bought fancy clothes to show how prosperous he was. Little did he know that those clothes made him look more like a gangster than a businessman.

He was also devoted to his church and family, and to the extended Greek community that had welcomed him in Worcester. If an old Greek song

15

George's family in Greece, c. 1918.
From the collections of Worcester Historical Museum

From 1960 to 1965, I worked at Wyman-Gordon Worcester. I became a regular customer and got to know George and Catherine. One of my earliest memories was back in 1960, when I was a truck driver. I went to the bar and George waited on me. I had a hot dog and a beer. I spoke with George and walked out without picking up my change. Two weeks went by before my next visit. I went to the bar. George waited on me. I had a hot dog and a beer. Then he went to a drawer, took out a bunch of bills and change, then placed them in front of me. I said to him, "What's that for?" He said, "You were in here two weeks ago and left without picking up your change from a $20 bill."

This is what he said to me: "If you cheat me, only you will know it. If I cheat you, everyone will know it." I could not believe it. I kept that in my mind all these years.

—John "Bill" Radzik, b. 1928

(Right) The former Wyman-Gordon building on Washington Street.

came on, he might cry because it reminded him of what he had left behind.

It was no wonder that my grandfather missed the old country. When he first came to the United States from Greece in search of the American Dream, he was only 16 years old. There were few prospects for him in his small farming village of Pikerni on the Peloponnese peninsula after World War I. George said goodbye to everything and everyone he loved, including his parents and younger siblings, after promising his father that he would send money back to Greece to support his family. Like so many immigrants to this country, he hoped to follow his dreams, better his chances in life, and earn enough money to support his family.

I met my husband, Jim, when I was 15 years old and he was 18. He played in a band called the Cactus Ramblers. I lived in Millbury, and he lived in Worcester. He would take the bus out to Millbury to pick me up, and then we took the bus back to Worcester to go to the movies, and then to Coney Island. First, we did this once a week, then twice, and it became three times a week before long! Jim went into the service in 1942, and returned home for a short furlough in December 1943. We were married that same month. He returned to service until the war ended in 1945. Coney Island was always a special place to us. Jim passed away in 1995, and every time I think of Coney Island, I think of him and all the time we had together.

—ISABELLE LUCILLE LYONS

(Left) Isabelle and Jim Lyons on their wedding day.

Interior of George's Coney Island.

George connected with friends and relatives living in Haverhill upon arrival in America in 1916.
From the collections of Worcester Historical Museum

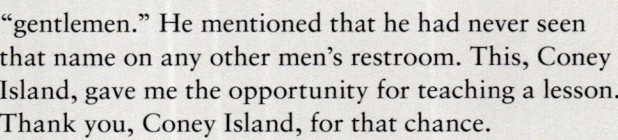

Many, many years ago, my 12-year-old grandson, Brian, and I would come into Coney Island for something to eat. On one occasion, he asked what "Gents" meant on the men's room door. I took the opportunity to explain to him that it was short for "gentlemen." He mentioned that he had never seen that name on any other men's restroom. This, Coney Island, gave me the opportunity for teaching a lesson. Thank you, Coney Island, for that chance.

—AL SCULTHORPE

A BOY CHASES THE AMERICAN DREAM

With his father's blessing, George borrowed $80 and booked his fare across the ocean aboard the *Vasilefs Constantinos*, the "King Constantine." I can't imagine what courage it must have taken for George and thousands of other immigrants to endure such a journey. The ship took a dozen days to travel from Greece to New York, and conditions for third-class passengers like my grandfather were dismal. He traveled in the bowels of the ship, where breakfast consisted of dried cookies with tea, with leftovers from the upper-class cabins served for both lunch and supper.

Recently, my son and I visited Ellis Island, New York, where my grandfather's ship arrived on June 15, 1916. I wept as I imagined how anxious he must have been, waiting in long lines for his physical examination with other immigrants from around the world, all of them trying to imagine what lay beyond those walls.

Many new arrivals were fearful, not only because they were in a completely foreign place and didn't speak the language, but because failing the exam meant they would be sent immediately back to their homelands. George was young and healthy, fortunately, and made it through. His certificate of arrival lists his name as "Georgios Tsagkarelis."

Upon their arrival, the immigrants were given apples and bananas to eat; many who hadn't seen bananas before ate them whole, peels and all. When George exchanged what little Greek currency he had for American money, he excitedly thought the pennies were made of gold and was reluctant to spend them.

From New York, George took an eight-hour train journey to Haverhill, Massachusetts, where he had a cousin. He moved into his cousin's boarding house, which had no heat except for a wood-burning stove;

George and his housemates slept fully clothed, right down to their shoes.

His first job was in a shoe store, painting hides and sweeping the floor for only $3.25 per week despite working long days. It wasn't much, but it was enough to keep George going, and he remained there until the business closed shop. He next found work as a dishwasher in a restaurant in exchange for meals, and after the supper shift he worked in a shoeshine parlor for a nickel an hour.

Despite the hardships he faced, George's entrepreneurial spirit remained strong, and in 1919 he opened a candy shop with his cousin in Salisbury Beach. At the end of the summer, instead of having made money, they found themselves in debt to the tune of $200 and George had to start over again.

Eventually, my grandfather bought his own shoe parlor on $1,400 credit. He sold it a year later for $2,800, but just as he was finally achieving financial stability, his younger brother died and George had to send his savings home to his family. Once again he was penniless. Dispirited, he returned to shining shoes.

(Left, top to bottom)
Vasilefs Constantinos, the "King Constantine."

Immigrants at Ellis Island in the early 20th century.

George and his cousin opened a short-lived candy shop in Salisbury Beach in the summer of 1919.
From the collections of Worcester Historical Museum

I'm 83 years old and have been going to Coney Island all my eating life. I credit Coney Island's two "up" hot dogs as being instrumental in me reaching this age. I shall continue to march towards 100 with their help. I have so many memories associated with this iconic establishment. Many other eating establishments have gone away with little remembrance of what made me go there in the first place. Anyone who goes to Coney Island remembers the ambiance of feeling like they are back in a better time, enjoying the friendly atmosphere on both sides of the counter.

—JEREMIAH ADAMS

Feltman's and Nathan's on Coney Island (New York) were first to sell sausage on a roll. In the early 20th century, the popularity of hot dogs spread to Detroit as the auto industry boomed.

Photo (bottom) Katherine Yung and Joe Grimm, *Coney Detroit*, front cover. Copyright © 2012 Wayne State University Press, with the permission of Wayne State University Press.

THE ORIGIN OF THE "CONEY DOG"

In the early years of the 20th century, while George was still living in the Greek village of Pikerni, a culinary evolution of sorts was taking shape in America.

Around 1870, on Coney Island, NY, German immigrant Charles Feltman began selling sausages in rolls. Years later, Polish immigrant Nathan Handwerker, who had been an employee of Feltman, opened his famous hot dog stand on Coney Island in 1916. By this time, Coney Island was one of the country's premier tourist destinations, drawing huge crowds in the spring and summer.

New waves of immigrants from Greece and Macedonia entered the U.S. in the early 1900s. Meanwhile the growing hot dog craze on Coney Island had spread inland, particularly in Michigan. As these immigrants entered through Ellis Island and moved inland, they brought their own twist to the growing food phenomenon they witnessed on New York's Coney Island.

Detroit was a boom town in the early 20th

As early as 1914, the Coney dog was born when chili sauce topped the traditional hot dog at places like Todoroff's Original Coney Island (Jackson, Michigan), Ft. Wayne's Famous Coney Island (Fort Wayne, Indiana), Lafayette Coney Island and American Coney Island (Detroit, Michigan) and, of course, George's Coney Island (Worcester, Massachusetts).

century as the burgeoning automobile industry attracted tens of thousands of workers to the assembly lines. Hot dogs were the perfect food for a growing industrial workforce on the go—fast, cheap, and easy to eat with your hands.

But the evolution of a particular manner of serving a hot dog, known as the Coney Dog was a product of this particular group of immigrants from Greece and Macedonia. Greek immigrants had already established a new culinary tradition based on chili in several U.S. cities, most notably in Cincinnati. At some point, as hot dogs grew in popularity, some of them introduced chili sauce to a hot dog.

In time, the Coney Dog came to be defined as a hot dog on a (steamed) bun topped with a beanless chili sauce, mustard, and chopped onions.

In Michigan, Coney Island hot dog stands and restaurants became part of the fabric of that state's culture. For years, Todoroff's Original Coney Island in Jackson claimed to have invented the Coney Dog in 1914. But that same year, Fort Wayne, Indiana, saw the opening of Ft. Wayne's Famous Coney Island Weiner Stand. Another claim to the original Coney Dog comes from Cincinnati, where according to local lore, the Coney Dog began with that city's legendary Greek chili parlors and its own Coney Island Amusement Park (founded in 1887 and named after the original in New York—and still open today).

In 1921, brothers Gust and Bill Keros, former shepherds from Greece, opened Lafayette Coney Island in downtown Detroit. But the brothers had a falling out, and Bill opened another restaurant next door.

The rivalry is legendary in Detroit making these two of the most famous Coney establishments in the country. Their individual recipes were as closely guarded as family heirlooms as is George's Coney Island's "secret sauce" is today.

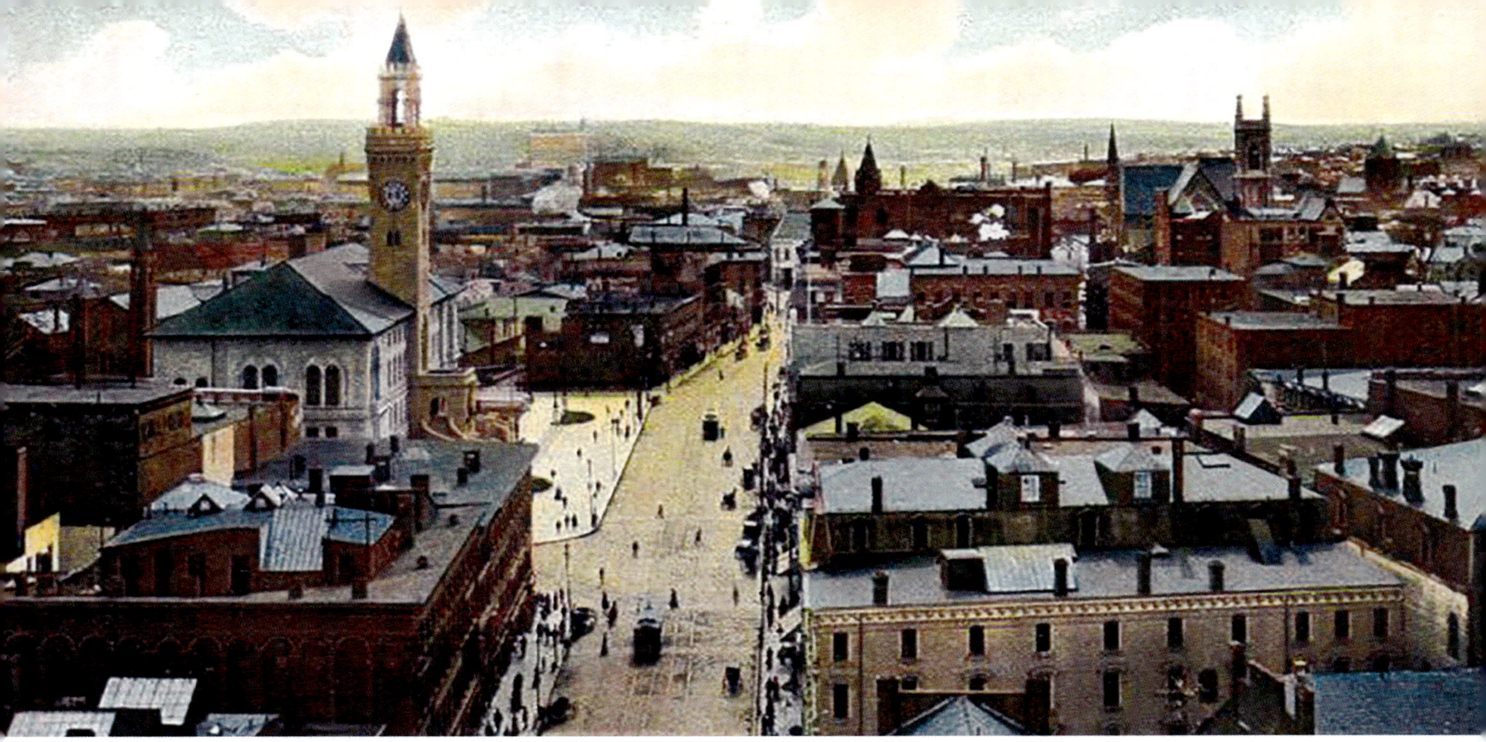

The Greeks, destined to form a large and strong group later in the century, had just begun to arrive (in 1900). In 1925, they moved into St. Spyridon's Church on Orange Street.

—From *Worcester: Heart of the Commonwealth*, by Margaret Erskine

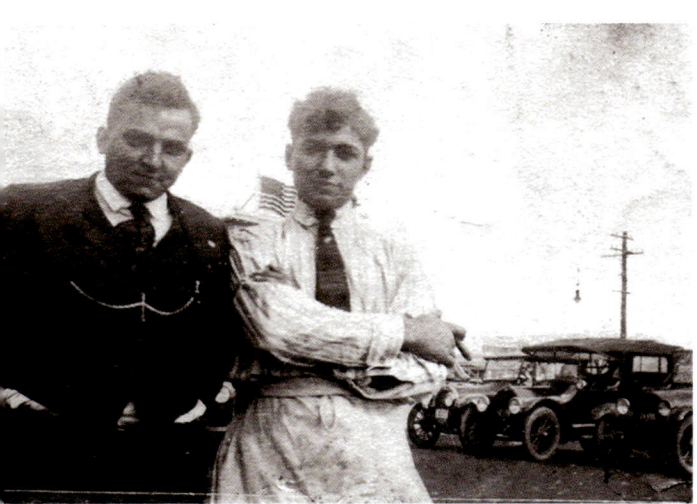

(Top) Worcester, Massachusetts, c. 1926.

(Bottom) George and friend in 1919 before moving from Haverhill.

Starting Over Again in Worcester

As he struggled to find opportunity in America, my grandfather went through many periods of acute apprehension and grief. At times he would even break down and cry. But George stayed on, driven by a duty to support his family back in Greece.

After exhausting his job options in Haverhill, my grandfather struck out for Worcester, a bigger and—he hoped—more prosperous city, where he had distant relatives. George was part of a growing group of immigrants who saw the potential for work in Worcester, which made its mark as a manufacturing center in the early 19th century. By 1926, Worcester's population had grown to nearly 190,000. About 70 percent of its residents were immigrants drawn to the plentiful jobs for workers who needed little education. The manufacturing companies included Washburn & Moen, American Steel & Wire, Morgan Construction, Norton Company, Royal Worcester Corset Company, and our neighbor, Wyman-Gordon.

In the second half of the 19th century, about half of the people living in Worcester were of Irish Catholic descent, but by the time George arrived,

Worcester was attracting immigrants from a broad spectrum of countries, like Armenia, Canada, Italy, Lebanon, Poland, Sweden, Syria, and, of course, Greece. The Greeks especially epitomized "the immigrant success story," according to historian Morris H. Cohen, author of *Worcester's Ethnic Groups: A Bicentennial View*. "Starting with no capital, they often set up a peanut, popcorn or fruit stand on the Common," he wrote. "Finally a number of them were able to open restaurants of their own."

George found work at Alpha Lunch Company on Main Street, where he made $20 weekly for six-and-a-half nights a week. In search of community and a connection with the old country, he became involved with St. Spyridon, the Greek Orthodox church established in Worcester in 1914, and began meeting others in the Greek community.

One of George's friends at the church was Dr. Anthony Vamvas, whose sister owned a luncheonette in the enormous Northridge Furniture building on Southbridge Street. The shop was modest, with only a handful of small wooden desk-chairs—the sort of chairs with side tables attached. Patrons would eat their meals in those chairs and move on quickly. One of the most popular lunches on offer was a hot dog with a special meat sauce.

When Dr. Vamvas discovered that his sister's health was failing, he offered to give George the chance to take over the luncheonette business. My grandfather jumped at it. Finally, a real opportunity to get ahead!

Unknowingly, George was buying into more than just the luncheonette. He also got that recipe for the secret sauce that helped make him—and his hot dogs—famous. In a nod to his arrival in New York, he renamed the tiny restaurant "George's Coney Island Luncheonette."

The restaurant he operated in those early years bears little resemblance to Coney Island today. It featured a full wait staff and a comprehensive menu, though even then there was an emphasis on "our famous Coney Island special hot wieners."

(Top) The Alpha Lunch Company on Main Street, Worcester.

(Bottom) St. Spyridon Orthodox Church on Orange Street.

From the collections of Worcester Historical Museum

(Top) George Tsagarelis behind the counter, c. 1930.

(Left) The Northridge Furniture building on Southbridge Street, c. 1900, was the original site of the sandwich shop George took over in 1924. The building burned in 1992. The current location of George's Coney Island is to the left of the former Northridge building.

He brought along one counterman, George O'Neil, who had worked with him at the Alpha. They worked 12 hours a day, seven days a week building up the business. Evidently they had a secret. There were five other similar establishments on Southbridge Street, between Madison and Herman Streets. They all went out of business within a few years.

—Roger Pierce
Worcester Telegram & Gazette

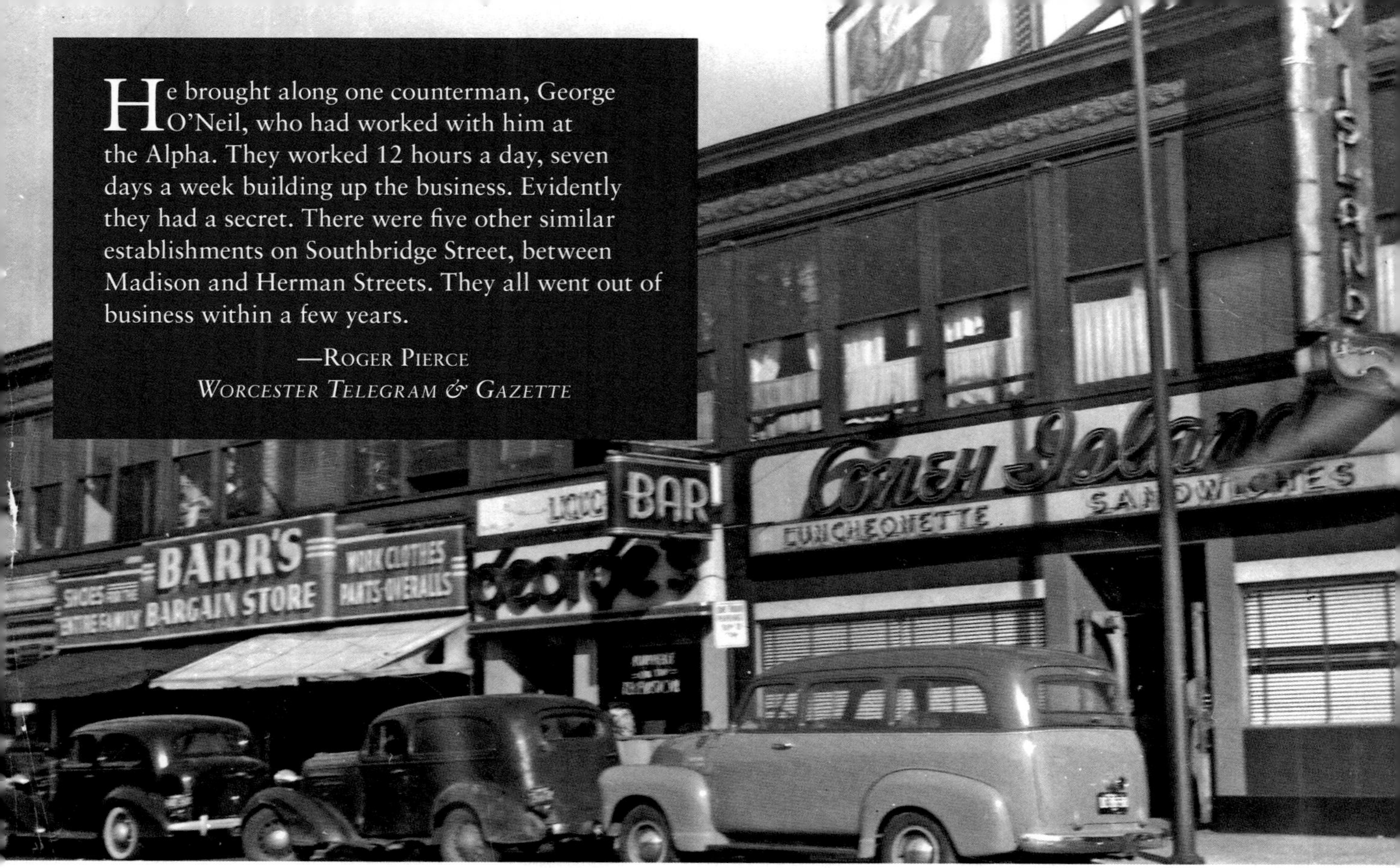

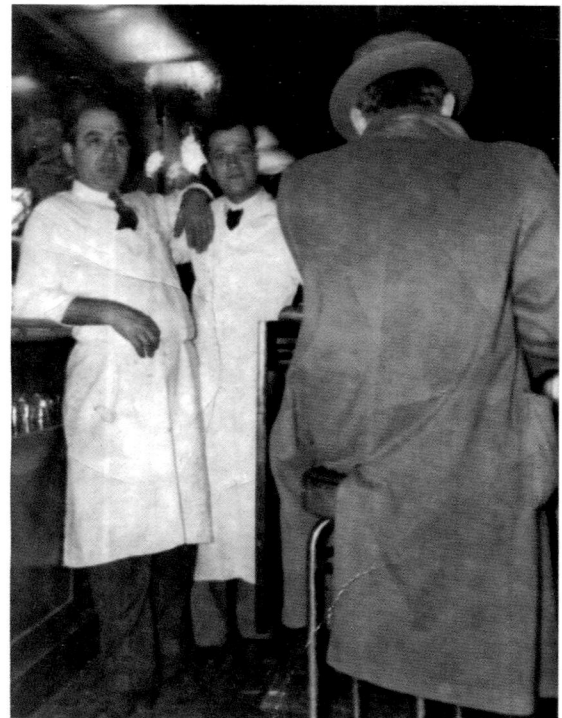

Photo (top) from the collections of Worcester Historical Museum

Moving Up in the World

Shortly after buying the business, George closed down the space in the Northridge building and moved the restaurant to its present location at 158 Southbridge Street. In fact, he initially had only half the space of the current establishment and added the bar section later. The back of the old brick building, built in the 1800s, had served as a blacksmith shop for the city's stable of horses. Horses were used to pull trolley cars until the advent of electricity, which led to electric trolley cars, making the stables and blacksmith shop obsolete.

In those early years, he faced another challenge when the building in which he was leasing space was put up for auction by its owner, the City of Worcester. A friend in the community once again stepped up to lend a hand. Matthew Whittall, a daily customer at Coney Island, was a rug manufacturer in the historic Whittall Mills.

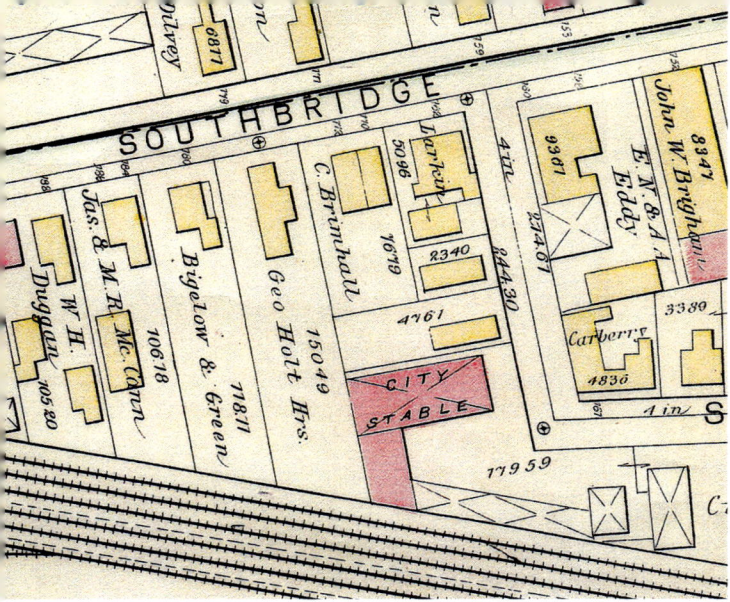

Worcester street map, 1882, showing the city stables behind the future site of George's Coney Island Luncheonette. The building at 158 Southbridge Street was built in the mid-1800s as a boarding house, and the lower back portion housed a blacksmith shop for the city stables.
From the collections of Worcester Historical Museum

I remember coming to Coney Island when I was 12 years old after we roller-skated at Mechanics Hall every Saturday and Sunday. Hot dogs were four for $1 at the time. George was the best. I never had enough money, being poor and getting $2 a week. He would give me four hot dogs and chocolate milk. Now I am in my sixties and I bring my grandchildren here. They love it. The waitresses always greet you with a smile, which means a lot. This place will always be remembered.

—DONNA STUBBET, B. 1957

An industrial complex off Brussels Street built between 1870 and 1930, Whittall Mills was originally the home of Crompton Rug Company and then the Worcester Carpet Company. At the time of World War I, Whittall was the largest employer in south Worcester, with 1,500 workers operating 350 mills in 500,000 square feet of factory space.

Whittall urged George to buy the building at auction. When George couldn't raise enough money in time, Whittall walked up to George and handed him the deed to the building, which he had bought at auction for $2,500. According to family lore, Whittall said, "George, the place is yours. Whenever you get the money, return it."

Despite the stock market crash of 1929, George managed to repay the loan and gain full ownership of the building by December 1933—just as the Great Depression descended on the country. But my grandfather was a survivor. There was no iconic sign looming yet over the city. Still, a legend had been born, and the message on George's menu in 1926 still rings true today: "You are Now in the Place Where Quality is Supreme."

Hot dogs keep 81-year-old young

LOOKING GOOD

Mrs. Tsagarelis glances up as her son-in-law, Father Solon Tsandikos, a priest with a Greek Orthodox church in Clinton, leans into the booth, saying affectionately, "Hey, she looks pretty good for an 81-year-old broad, don't you think?"

(Opposite page) Catherine Tsagarelis, age 81, and clippings from the *Worcester Telegram & Gazette* Closeup column, c. 1990.
Courtesy of the *Worcester Telegram & Gazette*

(Above) Catherine with Coney employee, Vickie Feliciano.

THE QUEEN OF CONEY ISLAND

One of the greatest opportunities of my life was working alongside my grandmother, Catherine, for many years. When I was a little girl, I used to love staying at her house. Either she or George would work late on weekends, and I would sleep over and watch movies with a remote control in her bedroom. This was a treat, because growing up, we didn't have TVs in our bedrooms, and we certainly didn't have a remote control.

On Saturday mornings, Catherine would go down Main Street to get her hair done at Gracie's. It wasn't fancy like salons today. This simple establishment was a second-floor walk up.

After the salon, Catherine would open Coney Island. I often went with her, and by being in the restaurant and helping her with odd jobs, I began learning the nuances of how to run the business. Catherine taught me the importance of paying attention to every detail, large and small.

Another of my favorite memories is how, every Saturday night after closing Coney Island, my grandmother would stop for the Sunday paper in the earliest morning hours on her way home so she'd have it to read with her coffee. Truthfully, I don't think she and my grandfather ever slept much.

My grandparents loved Coney Island the way most people love their children, and they put their hearts, souls, and countless hours of hard work into ensuring that the restaurant would thrive. This was the work ethic that Catherine and George passed down to our family, and to their employees, who they treated like family. Even on Tuesdays, her only day off, my grandmother would take us to the beach or for a drive, but no matter how late the hour or how tired she was, Catherine would always stop by Coney Island on the way home just to check in and make sure everything was set for opening the next day.

My grandmother taught me the business end of running a restaurant, showing me how to keep an inventory of supplies, how to do the accounts, and how to deal with licenses and inspections. More importantly, Catherine taught me how to interact with people and always make them feel welcome—a crucial skill if you're going to run a successful business.

She was smart, warm, socially adept, and generous—even hiring back employees my grandfather had fired from time to time, and always sharing food with those in need. She had a quick sense of humor, too, and really knew how to listen to people from all walks of life and make them feel valued, whether they were customers, clients, friends, suppliers, or employees.

As my own mother, Joanna, noted, Catherine had a special way about her. "Anybody could talk to her," she said. "She got along with everybody. It was amazing. So many of the regulars adored her, and she got to know all of them. Even if she couldn't remember a name, she could describe someone sitting at the bar. 'You remember him,' she'd say. 'He sat at the bar with the brown leather jacket, always had a beer and two hot dogs.' She could describe anyone we didn't know. That was her way."

It makes sense that my grandmother had such an ease about her at Coney Island. After all, she was the daughter of a successful restaurant owner, and she had grown up in the food business. My grandfather was lucky to have met her. They were a great team from the day they married.

Before that day, with no one special in his life, George had poured his energy into making the business a success despite the stock market crash that had sent Worcester and the rest of the country spiraling downward into the Great Depression. Then, in 1931, one of George's friends happened to see my grandmother singing in a choir in Bridgeport,

(Top to bottom) George and Catherine at work and on the town.

Catherine with daughter Joanna, c. 1945.

Connecticut, and reported to George that he had found the perfect girl for him. Soon, George was making trips between the two cities, dating my grandmother, Catherine, and running Coney Island. They were married in 1933.

The oldest of four children, Catherine was the daughter of Aristotle and Anastasia Angelopoulos and could understand George's long hours, since her parents owned three successful restaurants in Bridgeport. Still, those first years of married life were tough on her, since Catherine had left her friends and family behind and didn't know a soul in Worcester.

She was also a working woman at a time when most women didn't work outside the home. In the 1930s, only a quarter of U.S. women were gainfully employed, and most professional women worked as nurses or teachers. But Catherine was a force to be reckoned with; she had more energy than anyone else I've ever known. Soon after my mother, Joanna, was born, Catherine joined George at Coney Island and found her true calling behind the

With grandaughter Kathryn, c. 1990.
Courtesy of the *Worcester Telegram & Gazette*

31

I have fond memories of Catherine starting from the time I was seven years old. I remember walking from Armory Court to Lowe's Theater and asking my mother for extra money because I had to have a hot dog. Once, my mother did not have any extra. After the movies, I walked in and told Catherine I could not buy one, so she gave it to me for free. God bless her. I remember how just about everybody in the neighborhood knew each other. We used to walk from our homes to downtown on Saturday afternoon. There was a Newberry 5&10 and a Woolworths. Oh, the good old days.

—Alice Leahy, b. 1932

Thank you for all the tubes and brews I've had served to me by Catherine in the back bar. Don't believe we ever got charged full price. Thank you!

—Dan McCabe

counter. Her husband had been working hard since purchasing the luncheonette to grow the business, but Catherine—with her boundless generosity, sense of humor, and energy—played an essential role in keeping people coming back for generations.

My grandmother could talk to anyone and got along with everyone. She treated every single person who walked through the doors exactly the same. Whether it was a kid without a nickel for a hot dog or a well-dressed businessman, everyone was equal in her eyes. Newcomers were encouraged to come back, and regular customers adored her because my grandmother took time to get to know each and every person who came into the restaurant. She was also known for her generosity: if she saw people going hungry, Catherine always found a way to feed them.

To her, work was a second home. "My customers come in, we all know one another," she said. "We talk. We laugh. We have a ball."

Despite the long hours she put in at the restaurant, where she sometimes worked until three in the morning, Catherine found time for family, church, and friends. She liked her hot dogs well done with mustard and special chili sauce, and she ate one every day for 66 years.

She was truly a woman ahead of her time. When other Greek grandmothers were at home, baking baklava and spanakopita, Catherine was either running Coney Island or scooping us up and driving to Bridgeport or New York City or to the Cape for a swim—in her cherished Cadillac, of course. Catherine bought a new Cadillac every two years, in every color imaginable. It was a fitting car for a savvy businesswoman who truly embraced all of the love, laughter, and adventure that life has to offer.

Recently, one of our favorite customers paid me the ultimate compliment, saying, "Kathy, you're getting to be more like your grandmother every day."

I couldn't have felt more honored. I am so blessed to have had Catherine as a role model in my life, and I try to make her proud in all that I do.

Drawing of "Marna" (Catherine) and Kathryn Tsandikos by Kathryn's son, Solon Kelleher.

The Queen: Catherine Tsagarelis grills hot dogs at Coney Island, 1989.
Courtesy of the *Worcester Telegram & Gazette*

STAYING TRUE to our ROOTS

My first date with my husband was a movie. After, we drove to Coney Island. I was 16 and had never heard of the place. I refused to go inside so he went in and bought hot dogs to go. This went on for quite a few dates before I finally relented and went inside. Our order was always the same: two with no onions, three with sauce and onions, and two chocolate milks. This routine went on for the next 68 years once a week. In the late 1960s, I worked at the old post office that used to be near Coney Island. At break time, one of the clerks would go around and take orders for hot dogs. Nothing beats Coney Island hot dogs!

—Barbara Holohan

(Above) Staff at Coney Island, c. 1940.
(Opposite page) George Tsagarelis tends bar.

I remember looking up at the counter, not really knowing what a Coney Dog was. As I grew up, I came to order them all the time! The retro colors, graffiti benches, worn tables, and the iconic sign make this a Worcester landmark. I bring anyone I meet who's never been here to partake—including my parents. They were fans of the competitor on a hill to the west. I brought them over to the Coney side of my life. Ha! My earliest memory is when the lines would fill the entire restaurant, yet you were ordering within minutes.

—CHUCK McELROY, B. 1965

(Above) The interior with the jukebox added by George and Catherine.

(Inset) Tiles at the entrance.

(Right) Penny scale.

HOW CONEY ISLAND GOT ITS SIGNATURE LOOK

When you work in a place almost every day of your life, as I do at Coney Island, that place becomes so familiar that it's like a second home. I don't often take time to notice the décor that draws so many people here, like the porcelain enamel panels and Vitrolite glass, or the brushed steel letters and vintage bar. In fact, some days I only notice things like a light bulb that needs replacing.

Every now and then, though, I'll sit in one of our booths at Coney Island and think about how, in 1938, my grandparents bravely reinvested their profits in this restaurant and renovated the place completely, introducing an art deco décor that was so trendy and stylish at the time.

The maroon, brown, and black tiles installed on our floor are still here, including the ageless entrance tiles that form the word "Coney Island." So are the booths and tabletops. George and Catherine added a penny scale and a jukebox to give the place a playful feel, as if people might break out dancing at any instant.

OUR BELOVED BOOTHS

Perhaps more than any other aspect of Coney Island, our booths are a shrine to our relationship with our loyal customers, decorated with names, hearts, doodles, and sayings joyfully etched into the wood by generations of customers lovingly carrying on their family traditions and ours, too.

Wouldn't George and Catherine be amazed, if they saw the same booths they had installed now occupied by people on cell phones that connect them to the world?

(Above) The booths on the bar side remain pristine but the booths on the luncheonette side (below and opposite page) are carved with names from as far back as the 1930s.

One of the unique things about Coney Island is the way people have carved sayings, initials, and doodles on the wooden booths and walls. Many people come back to see the initials they wrote here long ago, perhaps inside a heart with the person they're married to now, or they bring their children and grandchildren to see their names and carve their own. These carvings are a testament to Coney Island love in all its forms.

Coney Island is famous through word of mouth, from people who have returned again and again. For me, the most striking are the writings and carvings on the booths that go back to the 1930s. Some just wrote their names, while others professed their love. You wonder how many thousands of names are written on the booths of Coney Island. This is why whoever is alive and running Coney Island can never touch those messages from our loyal clients.

—Fr. Solon Tsandikos

I remember writing my name on the wall (oops) when I was ten years old. Fifteen years later, I see my name on the same wall that I previously signed. I showed my son the wall, and he put his name next to mine. He was so excited. It's a memory he and I will never forget! Thank you, Coney Island!

—Anthony "TJ" Allen, b. 1976

When I was six years old, my parents and grandparents would always bring me and my siblings here for an outing. I know my name is carved in several booths. Now I bring my son here.

—Michael Ustaitis, b. 1969

When I was eight years old, my father would give me a nickel to play the jukebox. When I was 13, I came in with my girlfriend and we wrote our names in a booth table wall. Sorry about that. It looks like it caught on.

—Robert Grogan, b. 1958

When I was five years old, my nana took me and showed me where she and my grandpa carved their names in the seat. Every Friday as a teen, I came and had a hot dog. And, I still come here today.

—Nicholette Burrows

When I was young, I did not have enough money to go to Coney Island. I used to go to the Family Theater on Front Street and all I had left in my pocket was a little change. When I got older, I came here many times. I wrote my name on the wall, but now it is hard to find it. Some places you can eat off the floor. This place, you could eat off the ceiling. I enjoyed the hot dogs then and I still enjoy them now. Hope you stay open for many years.

—Ernie Lajoie

As a teenager, we went dancing at St. Mary's High School and stopped at Coney Island. We carved the names of our true loves on tables and booths. Back then, you knew that a boy loved you if you went to Coney Island and he carved your initials. Guys used to brag about how many hot dogs they could eat. When I worked at Wyman-Gordon, we would come for lunch. Now I bring my children and grandson to Coney Island and tell them my memories of the good ol' days. The restaurant hasn't changed, except for the digital jukebox.

—Anonymous, regular from 1963-69

An image from *American Squares* by Leah Frances. The book is based on an Instagram project that documents American cultural relics and iconography. See also p. 112.

I remember coming to Coney Island when I was six years old—and I am still coming. I remember coming down from Jefferson Street with my mom, dad, and brother on a Saturday afternoon for lunch—later watching the Army boys stop before getting on the trains, never realizing those boys may never come back.

—Barbara Tivnan, b. 1934

I started coming to Coney Island at age seven. Across from Coney Island was a railroad. My dad worked there as a freight handler. On payday, I would meet him on his lunch and go to Coney Island. The hot dogs, I believe, were 15 cents and two for 25 cents. Those were the good days! In my teens, I loved the jukebox.

—Patricia Burke Naple, b. 1944

(Above) Trains carrying soldiers from Fort Devens often unloaded troops on furlough, many of whom flocked to George's Coney Island for hot dogs and refreshments. The sign appears at the right edge of the photo. The station went out of service in the 1960s. The tracks are still visible but the structure is no longer there.
From the collections of Worcester Historical Museum

ALL ABOARD

Many of our customers have shared their fond memories of watching the trains arrive and depart from the station across the street from Coney Island. Worcester's history is closely entwined with the history of rail transportation, beginning with the first horse-drawn trolley cars rolling through Worcester during the Civil War.

By 1900, trains connected Worcester to other communities around Massachusetts, and even to other states. At its peak in 1916, the Worcester Consolidated Street Railway was the largest in Massachusetts, with more than 300 miles of track and 429 cars.

From 1903 to 1930, the Boston & Worcester Street Railway ran trains along 32 miles of track between Shrewsbury and Brookline. It only took two hours and 20 minutes to travel between the city halls in Boston and Worcester. Worcester Consolidated Street Railway began running both trolley and bus transportation in the 1940s; the last trolley left from Leicester to Worcester in 1945.

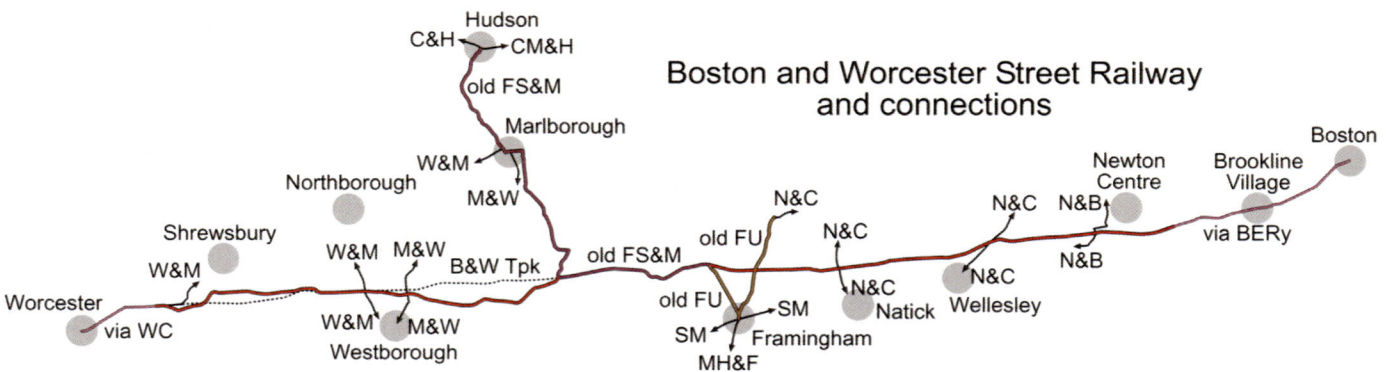

Boston and Worcester Street Railway and connections

I remember coming to Coney Island when I was eight years old. I would go with my father to shop at the market, then come here for lunch. We bought our first furniture at Northridge Furniture next door, and I remember waiting to see the trains go by. It was always a special treat to come here with my father. Whenever a group got together at home, off Hope Ave., it was the thing to go to Coney Island.

I once stopped in to talk with George and watched him cut the ends off each hot dog. Coney Island was my "Pit Stop." After high school, my girlfriends and I would stop in for one dog and chocolate milk (in a glass bottle). We sat behind the jukebox, carved our names, and played the 1950s music, like "Soldier Boy." We would take my daughter, who lives in New York now, to see the trains go by. Let's keep our memories alive and hope the next generation will come to make their own!

—Dorothy and Allyn Warren Krom, b. 1934

Buses eventually took over, along with private cars, ending the great age of rail transportation. The train station near Coney Island has been torn down, but we're happy to see that Union Station has been restored to its former glory. That train station, an increasingly busy commuter hub, is a reminder not only of Worcester's elegant architectural history, but of the many residents who once relied on trains and trolley cars to make their journeys.

(Above) The Boston & Worcester Street Railway and connections. Streetcars last operated on June 10, 1932, after which buses ran due to reconstruction of Route 9 as a major route.

(Right) Worcester's Union Station, restored and reopened in 2000, is one of the successes of urban preservation. It currently serves MBTA commuter rail lines between Worcester and Boston. Photo by Dany Pelletier

My grandfather took the train to Worcester from Boston on his way to fight in World War II. They stopped in Worcester to pick up some more soldiers. While they were waiting, he walked from Union Station to Coney Island with a bunch of guys. Long story short, after the war my grandfather came back time and time again, always with my father in tow, a little kid. He absolutely loved the place and drove out from Boston to eat there all the time. Later, my father, then in his early twenties, after a couple of tours in 'Nam, went back and ran into what would become my uncles. Long story short, he and my ma got together in part because of Coney Island. It truly is a landmark in Worcester, and to be honest, I might not be here today if it wasn't for that place. It is the essence of America, in my opinion.

—JUSTIN SOUZA

In the 1950s, I rode the train from Framingham to Rochester, NY. The train went by the back of the building with the sign printed on the building. All I knew of Worcester was Coney Island. I moved to the area in the early 1960s and met my wife. I have brought our children and grandchildren here.

—JOHN BOWER, B. 1946

When I was six years old, my parents, siblings, and I would come when we visited my grandmother on Vernon Hill. We used to take the Buddliner train from Webster and get off at the station directly across the street. That is a big change! The hot dogs are still as good as they were my whole life! My children and wife love Coney Island and get just as excited as I did when I was a kid.

—JOHN SENDROWSKI, B. 1960

Working behind the counter now looks pretty much the same as it did in George's day. Photo by Mike Henderickson

When I was ten years old, a group of boys walked from Southgate St. to the Ionic Ave. Boys Club every Saturday. After swimming and a movie, we came down the hill, got two dogs and a chocolate milk. You still have the original chair, but the one thing you should still have is the counter top with the big groove from cutting the hot dogs!

—John Daniel, b. 1943

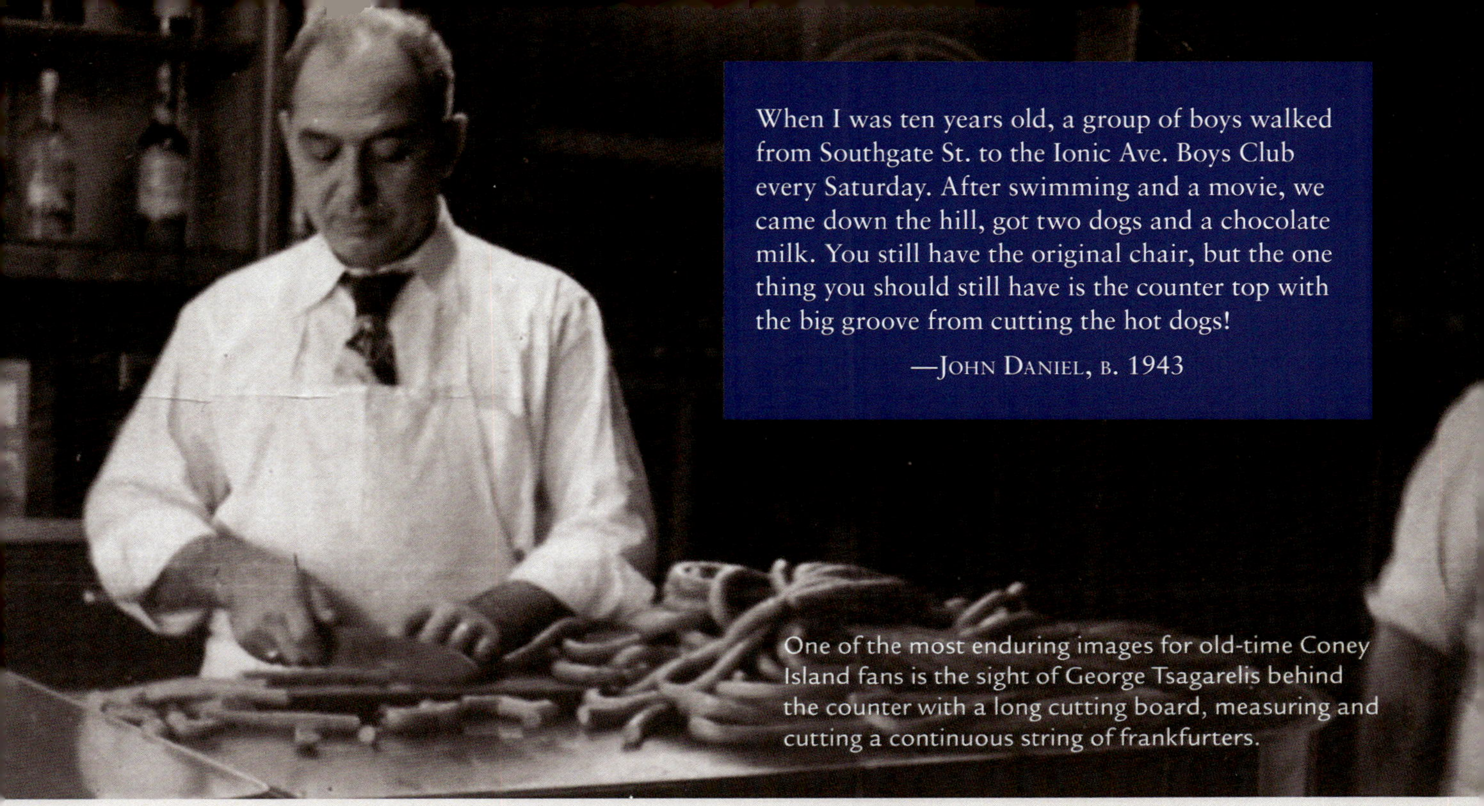

One of the most enduring images for old-time Coney Island fans is the sight of George Tsagarelis behind the counter with a long cutting board, measuring and cutting a continuous string of frankfurters.

My mother and I often walked from Coney Island to our house on College Hill. Sometimes we'd take the bus, but this was a walking city back in the day. My father would go down to the store at 11 a.m. and work until early evening, have dinner, and then go home and nap a little bit. He'd leave the house again about eleven o'clock at night, and go back to the store until two or three o'clock in the morning. My mother was there all during the day.

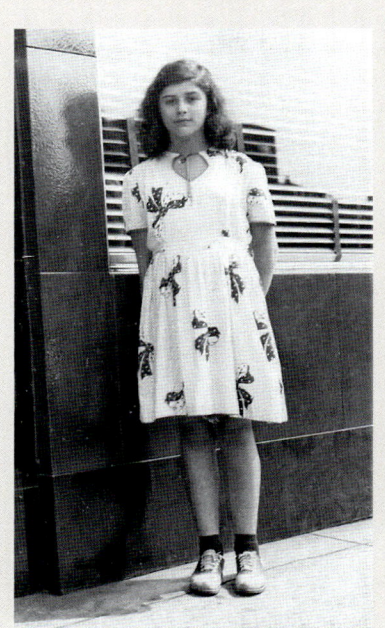

As I got older, I started going to school. Wherever I was, I had to be at Coney Island at six o'clock for dinner. I ate in the last booth at the back of the restaurant. Then my mother and I would go home. On many nights she would pack me up in my robe and pajamas, and we would go down to Coney Island in the middle of the night. We'd stop at the Waldorf, which was on Main St., where the Salvation Army is now. There was a cafeteria there, and we would go and eat in the early morning hours, and then pick up my father and go home as a family.

—Joanna Tsandikos, George and Catherine's daughter

(Left) Joanna Tsandikos

I remember coming to Coney Island when I was a teenager. In the 1950s, Coney's hot dogs were 15 cents, so we really splurged at Coney Island for 25 cents! Dropping our dates on Saturday night, and the guys meeting at Coney bragging (sometimes not truthfully) that we scored! The cold bottles of chocolate milk and the counterman using an ice pick to open the paper top.

—RICHARD RENIERE, B. 1936

I remember coming to Coney Island when I was 18 years old. My husband and I came here during World War II. We have our names somewhere on the wall. I am 94 years old now, and I just got a delicious hot dog for supper.

—IRENE ALUKAS, B. 1923

WORLD WAR II AND THE BOOM YEARS

The vibrant new Coney Island sign ushered in a boom period at the restaurant as World War II brought manufacturing jobs back to Worcester. Downtown once again became a beehive of activity as the train depot brought in soldiers passing through Worcester on their way to Fort Devens or other destinations.

The war years brought in a huge volume of business to the restaurant, especially in the evenings, when Coney Island was open until the early morning hours. George and Catherine both worked seven days a week on a staggered schedule.

Catherine worked days and George took double shifts. As soon as the U.S. officially entered the war in 1941, prices went up, according to my grandmother, who said that "frankfurts came in casings and my husband used to lay them on this big board and measure and cut them." George once described to a newspaper reporter how he purchased hot dogs in 30-foot strips and cut them 12 to a pound.

(Left) Table Talk pies are stacked near a carving in a Coney Island booth.
(Below) Basic training at Fort Devens, c. 1941.

During the World War II years, Coney Island became a destination for young people to gather and hear news about their friends enlisted overseas. The restaurant was always busy. In this photo George Tsagarelis takes a much-deserved break, c. 1941.

My mother and father met in 1940 on a blind date at Coney Island. My mother grew up in Worcester and came to Coney Island with her friends all the time. My parents were married on June 7, 1941 in Worcester. My father was in the Navy during World War II. When they came back to Worcester, the first place they ate at was Coney Island because that's where they first met. I always came here regularly growing up and I brought my children here as well. It's our family tradition. If it wasn't for Coney Island, I wouldn't have been born.

—JOANNE SCOTT JIJON, B. 1951

I lived in Worcester from 1959 to 1975 (South High, Class of '72). Coney Island was always a part of any South Worcester citizen's life. I recall taking my first dates there back in the wild 1960s. The carving-laden booths ooze a history of love lives past.

My favorite stories of Coney Island are from my deceased father-in-law, Mack (Neil) MacNeil. We would stop by there for a few cold ones and he would tell me of his younger days at Coney Island. He told me that, before and after WWII, Coney Island was the place to meet to find your friends. As the war started and all the young men were joining the armed forces, they would go to Coney Island to get news of who was going where for the war effort. After the war, all the Worcester County boys would go to Coney Island to find out what happened to their friends who went off to war. Were they dead or alive?

—KEITH LaROSE

When I was 7, my family took me to watch the circus break down. They used elephants then—paraded to Garden St. to load all on the train. Then, I got taken to Coney Island. What a big shot I thought I was, eating a hot dog way after dark! My six kids also have memories of coming here after rollerskating at Mechanics Hall. Coney Island, a treat for all!

—EDDIE TRAVER LEBOEUF, B. 1939

George and I were talking and drinking beer together one night, and he told me that he wanted a new sign. He wanted something different and something unusual. I watched George and noticed how he would hand a hot dog in a roll to a customer. I saw some mustard drip out and I got the idea of what the sign should look like. We never discussed a price; he just told me to come up with the idea and a handshake was enough. You know, that Coney Island sign, as it was in its full glory when I finished with it, it is my favorite. I created it for a man who appreciated it, a man who was my friend.

—STANISLOV ROMANOFF
from an article by Joanna Zikos
WORCESTER TELEGRAM & GAZETTE
January 22, 1984

(Above) Stanislov Romanoff, owner of the Master Sign Company, designed and built the iconic Coney Island neon sign.

THAT ICONIC SIGN

Like the Citgo sign in Boston, one of Worcester's most iconic landmarks is our neon Coney Island sign, which has been painted and photographed more times than I can count. During their honeymoon, my parents visited the Louvre in Paris, and claimed they saw a picture of Coney Island's sign hanging there!

It's true that our sign is pretty hard to miss. Besides being neon and bright, it depicts a hand holding probably the biggest hot dog you've ever seen. One of the first questions new customers ask is "Where did the sign come from?" Like everything to do with Coney Island, there's a lot of history involved—and friendship, too. Here's the story.

A few years after opening his business, George met Stanislov Romanoff, a Russian immigrant who came to America in 1912, four years before George. Their shared experience as strangers in a new land led to a warm friendship that endured many years.

Romanoff had studied architecture back in his native Kiev. He had come to the U.S. planning only to earn a little work experience before returning home, but in 1917 the Bolshevik Revolution changed everything. Instead of going back, he found a job at American Optical in Southbridge, where he worked for a few years before moving to Worcester.

He started his sign business, Master Sign Company, on a whim after the owner of the Island Market asked him to paint a sign for his storefront. Neon lighting revolutionized the sign industry after neon lights were first introduced at the Paris Motor Show in 1910, and Romanoff claimed to have designed and installed Worcester's very first neon sign in 1920 for Arkus Pharmacy on Water Street. He made neon signs for various other Worcester businesses, too, before designing three different signs for George's Coney Island between 1940 and 1951.

A young Joanna Tsagarelis stands on the corner beneath the first neon sign created by Stanislov Romanoff, c. 1940.

I remember old Worcester, window shopping from one end of the city to the other. In 1948, I remember being in a stroller with Mom while she was shopping at the market on Lincoln St. and School St. We walked down from the Lincoln Square Boys Club while window shopping. It was great. I've been coming here ever since to support a family business—and to admire the sign!

—Edward Crockett

Our car just can't go by here. It automatically stops. Jay worked as a sales rep for years. We need one in New Hampshire.

—Jay and Audrey, b. 1932 & 1933

The sign hanging up now is actually the third of Romanoff's creations for George's restaurant. The original one was over sixty feet tall, and featured neon lettering spelling out the name of the establishment. A few years later, it was replaced with a similar sign featuring an image of a dog chasing a hot dog. (Sadly, no photos of this second sign have been located to date.)

The current sign, for which George paid Romanoff $10,000, was installed on June 5, 1951. The fifty-foot neon masterpiece created a buzz in the city from the moment it went up. Over the years it has become a beacon for hot dog lovers all over New England.

Through the years, weather has taken a toll on the wires and neon tubing. Repair crews have visited the restaurant many times to refurbish the sign. In 1997, when the sign was removed by workers from Kay Gee signs in Auburn to be repaired in their

On Saturdays starting in 1930, my dad would bring me and my younger sister as a "treat." We would walk and keep an eye out for the "Dripping Hot Dog." My dad enjoyed a beer. It seems everything has changed; so much has been torn down."

—Madeleine, b. 1926

workshop, loyal Coney Island clients experienced a near panic. We had to reassure everyone that not only was Coney Island staying in business, but the sign would be back, good as new.

When I think about our sign, it doesn't just symbolize my second home, Coney Island's history, or my family's legacy. Our sign is a testament to the success of two hardworking immigrants from very different parts of the world and the bond of friendship that lasted a lifetime.

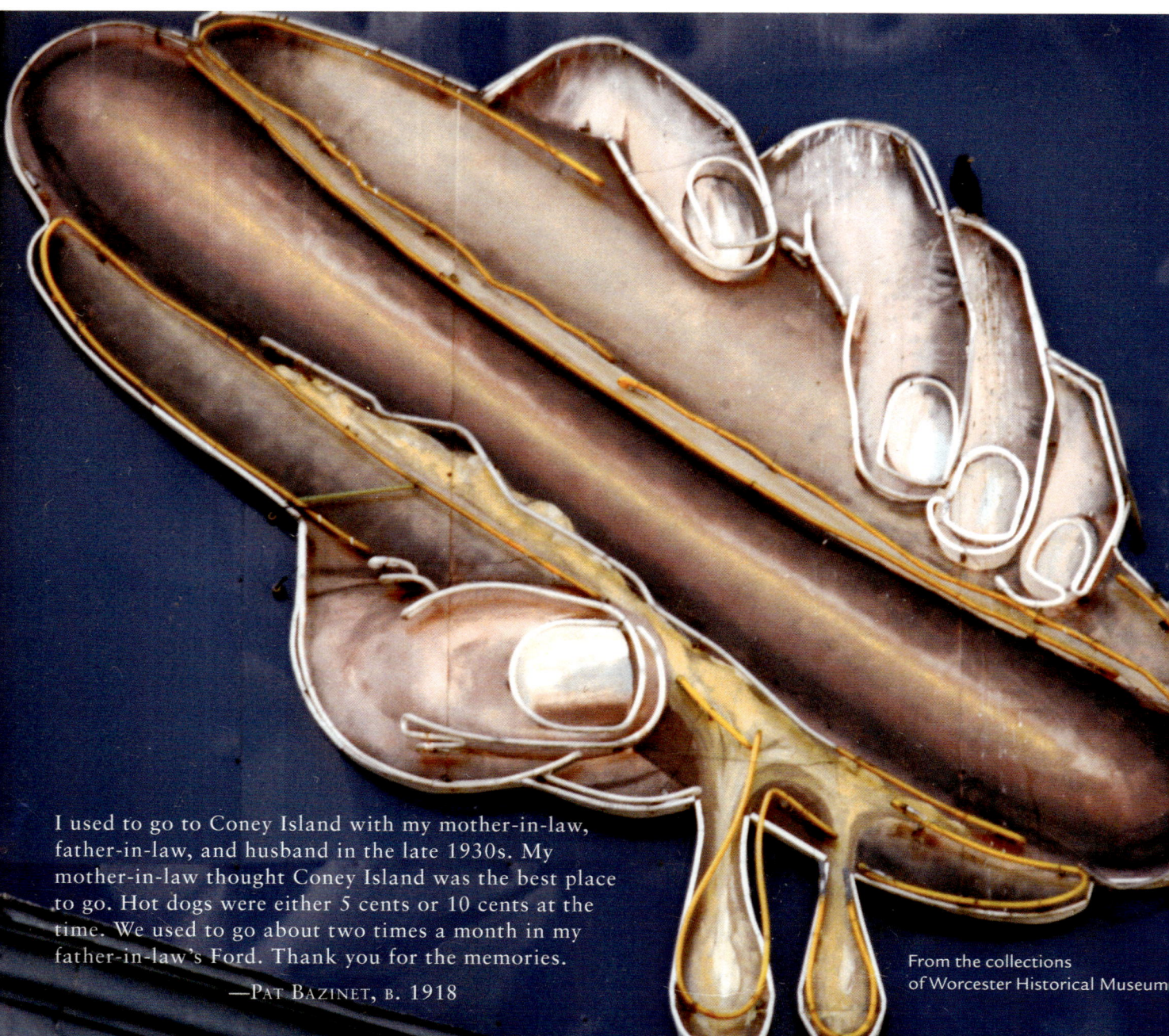

I used to go to Coney Island with my mother-in-law, father-in-law, and husband in the late 1930s. My mother-in-law thought Coney Island was the best place to go. Hot dogs were either 5 cents or 10 cents at the time. We used to go about two times a month in my father-in-law's Ford. Thank you for the memories.

—Pat Bazinet, b. 1918

From the collections
of Worcester Historical Museum

Installation of the sign, 1951.

"Repair work creates scare at Coney Island" (right) reads a subtitle in the *Worcester Telegram & Gazette*. In 1997 customers, who witnessed the sign being taken down and transported for repair, were concerned that their favorite restaurant was closing.

My father and I came to Coney Island before the war. I've taken all four of my children here, all nine of my grandchildren, and my five-year-old great-grandson. This is always a place to come in, keep warm and get a smile.

—Donald Baker

I love to come to Coney Island, not only for my favorite chili hot dogs, but also to enjoy the great Coney Island hot dog sign outside. A Worcester landmark!

—Susan Ceccacci

'People have been coming in all day wondering if we were closing down.'

KATHRYN TSANDIKOS

Doggone it! Where's the sign?

Repair work creates scare at Coney Island

By Bronislaus B. Kush
Telegram & Gazette Staff

WORCESTER — The familiar white-aproned "countermen" were on duty.

The special chili sauce was simmering.

The "chocklit" milk was on ice.

And the hot dogs, as usual, sat waiting to be tucked into the split, steamed rolls.

But many regulars at Coney Island Lunch could only think the worst.

The mecca for wiener lovers — open since the doughboys returned home from the battlefields of World War I — was shutting down.

After all, why had management pulled down the giant hot dog sign that had beckoned — with its dazzling neons lights — thousands of tube steak lovers into the art deco style eatery?

'A LITTLE WORRIED'

"Yeah, I was a little worried," said Tad Billery, who occasionally stops for lunch at the historic frankfurter joint before heading to work at the Worcester Common Outlets. "I see these guys pulling down the sign, and I figure that's it for the place."

Hot dog lovers, your taste buds can rest easy.

You won't have to switch to burgers.

The folks who run Coney Island have had problems off and on with the landmark sign for some time and have decided to fix it once and for all.

"People have been coming in all day wondering if we were closing down," said Kathryn Tsandikos, who runs the business her grandfather, the late George Tsagarelis, bought in the

Turn to NEON/Page A7

Ken Hart removes a piece of the Coney Island sign that will be refurbished and reinstalled.

DAN GOULD

51

A photo clipped from a travel magazine and framed is a permanent fixture in one fan's bathroom.

Over 40+ years my family and I have enjoyed your hot dogs! I also enjoy oldies music, so I found an oldies music shower curtain and bath accessories at Kohl's. I needed an oldies picture to hang in my bathroom.

One day, I was flipping through a travel magazine and laughed, as your Coney Island sign was in it! Your beautiful, crisp and clear photo was picture perfect! Over the years, every time I change my bathroom accessories and see your picture I smile as I remember the happy times eating and listening to your jukebox with my family!

—A Fan

• •

I have been coming to Coney Island for 72 years. The neighborhood wasn't so open. Lots of buildings and businesses have gone. Some of my friends and I used to come here every Saturday night after we went to a movie. We would walk about three miles. My sister called me "Pickles" because I always took a pickle to go. My wife used to go with me when we were first dating. After World War II, we got married. We lived on West St. for 30 years. Then we built a house in Sterling and lived there for 30 years. Then we moved to Ellenton, Florida. Your hot dogs bring me back to see family. I had four hot dogs today. They're still the best hot dogs around.

—William Lohnroth, b. 1926

Andrew Kelleher shows off one of Coney Island's signature hot dogs, c. 1993.

Courtesy of the *Worcester Telegram & Gazette*

Founders of Hopfmann Bros. in Clinton, Massachusetts: (from left) Alwin, William, and Ernest Hopfmann.

The dogs came in giant 70-lb. links. The time consuming thing for my father-in-law was cutting the hot dogs. He had a long cutting board. All day long, and all night long, he was cutting these hot dogs the size to be sold. He just measured and cut. Measured and cut.

—FR. SOLON TSANDIKOS
GEORGE AND CATHERINE'S SON-IN-LAW

Who invented the Coney Dog? Unfortunately, that's lost in history. The problem is that back then they didn't really keep any records. I don't think that people really thought it was that special because it was just a hot dog that Greek immigrants had been selling. As far as Joe and I could assert from our research, a number of Greek and Macedonian immigrants came to the U.S. and created the Coney Dog. It's very strange because they don't eat hot dogs in Greece, but they came and they concocted their own version of the American hot dog.

—FROM CONEY DETROIT
BY KATHERINE YUNG AND JOE GRIMM

A HAVEN FOR HOT DOG LOVERS

For years, my accountant has been saying, "You'd save so much money if you put up a soda dispenser." Others have suggested using paper plates instead of our heavy white dishes to save money on water and time on washing.

Some changes have been inevitable. George used to have to stand at the counter and cut up hundreds of hot dogs a day. Now they come in links. Rolls used to arrive at Coney Island in big boxes, and now they're delivered in plastic bags. Bottles of soda came in wooden cases, and now we have cans.

But you can't change things simply to make money or save time. As my hardworking grandparents demonstrated, that's not how you build a loyal customer base and a business that lasts. We have always tried to maintain the essence of Coney Island—that family-friendly, homey feeling—remaining as authentic to our roots as possible.

(Above) As teenagers in the 1960s, Dr. Peter Garofoli (on left) and Jack Graves used to deliver rush orders of Hopfmann frankfurters to George's Coney Island.

(Below) Kayem factory workers.

Courtesy of Kayem Foods, Inc.

From serving Worcester's own Polar soda and Table Talk Pies to our secret sauce, from offering bottles of chocolate milk to Wachusett potato chips, we are dedicated to staying true to our roots.

That's especially important when it comes to our hot dogs. We believe, as my grandparents did, that quality really matters. George relied on local, family-owned shops to supply the hot dogs for his growing business. In the early days, he made his Coney dogs with frankfurters from Hopfmann Brothers in Clinton, Massachusetts. Founded by German immigrants Alwin, William, and Ernest Hopfmann, their business was key to George's success in the early years, partly because they were always ready to fill a rush order if George ran low on supplies.

Dr. Peter Garofoli, grandson of Alwin Hopfmann, remembers working at the butchery beginning at age fifteen, saying, "Tuesday was slaughtering day. They brought the pigs in by a rail spur located near the rear of the building. We'd load about 400 lbs. of meat and spices into a compressor and then stretch the casing over a nozzle and fill it under pressure. Then we linked the dogs, stretched them over a rack, and then they went into the smoke-house. A hot dog straight out of the smoker was better than a T-bone steak!"

On many occasions, Garofoli and his friend Jack Graves would load 70 lbs. of cased meat from Hopfmann Bros. into the back of his father's car and make an emergency run to Worcester when Coney Island called. Other times, George would dispatch Catherine and their daughter to complete the mission.

George was the only customer who didn't want the hot dogs linked. Instead, he cut them himself. When he called and said he was running low, everybody jumped to attention.

—Dr. Peter Garofoli

George also bought hot dogs from Weigert's. Founded by German immigrant Harry Weigert, the Worcester-based butchery and store held its own iconic status in central Massachusetts during the first half of the 20th century. Sadly, like many small butcher shops, both Hopfmann Bros. and Weigert's went out of business in the late 1960s due to increasingly stringent and costly regulations imposed by the FDA, and we had to scramble to find new suppliers.

For the past half-century, George's Coney Island hot dogs have been made with Kayem hot dogs—made with beef and pork—from Kayem foods in Chelsea, Massachusetts. Kayem is a fourth-generation family business established by the Monkiewicz family in 1909.

So many of our suppliers have been local and family-owned, with the same work ethic my family possessed. We at Coney Island have been honored to do business with all of them:

We started doing business with Coney Island around 1968, not long after I returned from the army. I remember pulling up to the store for the first time and saying to myself, "Wow, this little rinky-dink place, I can't believe how many hot dogs they go through! Thousands per week!" The volume, yeah! I met George and his wife Catherine that day and we chatted for a while. I remember it was very nice. They wouldn't let me leave until I had a hot dog. My uncle used to say, "Don't ever take anything from a customer ... pay for it." They would not let me pay for that hot dog. So I had to break the rule that my uncle gave me. What was I supposed to do? My next memory of Coney Island was Father Solon. He spent a lot of time in the store, and was a friendly, welcoming presence. Our relationship with Coney Island has always been treated with special care at Kayem Foods. We are both family businesses, and that means a lot to us.

—RAY MONKIEWICZ

BROCKERT BREWING CO.

GREENWOOD DAIRY

HENRY FREEMAN & COMPANY

HOPFMANN BROTHERS

KAYEM

POLAR BEVERAGES

SALMON BROTHERS

H. E. SHAW TOBACCONISTS

TADCASTER ALE

TOWN TALK BREAD

WEIGERT'S

I remember coming to Coney Island when I was 12 years old. I used to come here after school (Sacred Heart) and sometimes with my brothers, sisters, mom, and dad. I remember having the chocolate milk in the bottles. Now I'm coming here with my children and grandchildren to carry on the tradition. The hot dogs are still great. Thank you for keeping it the way I remember it!

—Liz Cote Goodall, b. 1950

Photos this page and opposite courtesy of Kayem Foods, Inc.

If you know my dad, you'd know what a nut he was for hot dogs. He grew up in a small town in the Catskills that had a Texas Lunch. He loved that Texas Lunch, which is still there in that same small town today. He even perfected his own chili sauce. It was a secret, of course.

Back in 1985, my husband and I purchased our first house in Worcester. We had a lot of work to do on the house before we could move in. Each Friday night after work, my mom and dad would meet us at the house, where we'd tackle repairs on one room at time. After a few hours of work, the plan was that my dad would go out to get something to eat for us all and we'd break around eight.

The first night my dad made it back to the house after a lengthy hunt for a decent restaurant with takeout. He opened the back door, holding something in a covered Kayem hot dog box. He was so excited, and out of breath, like a little kid at Christmas. He told us about finding this great hot dog place not too far from the house. It was called George's Coney Island. Since the house was void of furniture, we put down a blanket on the floor and sat down to have an indoor picnic. My dad opened a full box and started handing out Coney Island hot dogs to each of us. It was just like Christmas! The smell of the onions, the chili sauce, and mustard started to fill the entire house. Heaven!

Although we ate most of the box of hot dogs, there were a few left for my mom and dad to take home, and I'm sure those dogs never saw the light of the next morning. Each time my parents came for a visit, my dad always had a full Kayem box of Coney Island hot dogs. I still see my dad's excitement with each dog. Now, 31 years later, my husband and I continue the tradition of bringing our children and grandchildren to George's Coney Island each time we're in Worcester.

—Julie Wilcox

● ● ● ● ● ● ● ● ● ● ●

You could get four hot dogs for a buck in 1957. It's like an art exhibition. (Watch out, Worcester Art Museum!)

—Bill Hughes

It was so good to visit Coney Island again after many years away. It had been 65-75 years. All the old timers who used to go with me have gone from the area. I was the kid of the group back in 1935 and 1936. Boy, were the hot dogs and chocolate milk good. Best around for miles. We would decide what we wanted while riding down to Coney Island and one person ordered for all of us. They were placed in a flat box with our chocolate milk. Those were the days. Two or three dogs were easy to down. The hot dogs today are just as good. Keep up the good work.

—TED T.

I remember coming to Coney Island when I was 16 years old. My sister, Ellen, and I would come here and each order six hot dogs and a chocolate milk. The hot dogs were 15 cents each. I still come to Coney Island. My grandchildren have even carved their names on the booths there.

—DAVID NORDSTROM, B. 1945

In 1954, my neighborhood friends would go around and collect orders for Coney Island hot dogs. We would occasionally get free dogs from George for getting the orders.

—GEORGE COTE, B. 1947

I started coming to George's over 50 years ago. We would travel here from Putnam, CT. I have never had such good Coney Island hot dogs. They are better than Nathan's in Coney Island. We now live on Long Island. Keep everything the same!

—ANONYMOUS, B. 1951

I remember coming to Coney Island with the family when I was eight years old. I believe at that time you served Weigert hot dogs from Greenwood Street in Worcester and Greenwood Dairy chocolate milk. I love bringing relatives from Australia to Coney Island because there is nothing like it there.

—DAVID KOWALCHEK B. 1963

I remember coming to Coney Island when I was 17 years old. There were four of us who played basketball until the lights at the park were shut off. We always came here afterwards. It was a great finish to the night. I challenged my friend, Jimbo, to eat as many hot dogs as he could and we would pay. If I remember correctly, he ate 11, our all-time record.

—MICHAEL, B. 1958

When I was around six years old, I used to deliver Kayem hot dogs to this restaurant with my grandfather, Anthony F. Dailida. When he was delivering hot dogs, I would eat two dogs with onions, mustard, and relish with a chocolate milk.

—KEVIN DAILIDA, B. 1970

My husband is from the Chicago area and is a "Chicago-dog" snob. I took him to Coney's when he moved here, and he loves the sauce—you made a believer of him!

—KELLEY MANSON, B. 1979

George was fiercely protective of the secret recipe to his chili sauce. Courtesy of the *Worcester Telegram & Gazette*

The first memory I have of Coney Island is being there as a youngster. My parents said that I was raised in a back room in a crib in the office. But I remember my first tricycle, which they bought me, and I used to ride around Coney Island with my tricycle. I also remember sitting on top of a shelf in the back room. I would sit there with my dad while he made the sauce.

—Joanna Tsandikos

People often ask if we're affiliated with Coney Island in New York. As discussed earlier, the "Coney" is a type of hot dog.

To recap, hot dogs in the United States date back to 1870, when German immigrant Charles Feltman began selling sausages in rolls on Coney Island. The first actual hot dog stand opened on Coney Island in 1916. Hot dogs became the perfect food for a growing industrial workforce on the go by the early 20th century, because they were fast, cheap, and easy to eat without utensils.

Meanwhile, new waves of Greek and Macedonian immigrants were entering the U.S. in the early 1900s. They established a new culinary tradition of chili, especially in Cincinnati, and at some point somebody decided that adding chili to a hot dog would be a great idea. The Coney dog was born, defined as a hot dog in a steamed bun topped with chili sauce, mustard, and chopped onions.

Everyone agreed on only one thing: that no single ingredient of a Coney dog is more important than its sauce. Some call it chili sauce. Others describe it as a beanless meat sauce.

The sauce featured in George's famous Coney dogs was made from a secret recipe created by Dr. Vamvas' sister, and when George bought her business, he promised that he would keep the recipe a secret. He did, guarding it as fiercely as a Doberman, other than confessing to a bit of tinkering with the sauce over the years and sharing it on a "need to know" basis with members of his family.

Catherine eventually took over the important job of making the sauce several times each week in batches large enough to keep the Coney dogs smothered. She, too, guarded the recipe with vigor, even snubbing a popular national culinary magazine that asked the question which should never be asked.

Catherine related the story to *Yankee* magazine in 1985: *Gourmet* magazine had once asked, "Would you mind sending us the recipe for your sauce?"

My grandmother's response was definitive: "I threw their letter in the wastebasket. Everybody knows it's the 'mystery sauce.' I wouldn't give it out at any price."

Catherine did eventually pass the recipe down to me, and the sauce is still lovingly made several times each week. It requires over 300 lbs. of meat to make it during an average week. People ask me all the time if I'll share the ingredients, but that's never going to happen.

(Left) Stirring the "secret" sauce, 2019.
Photo by Dany Pelletier

(Below) Kathryn Tsandikos "dresses" hot dogs, c. 1990.
Courtesy of the *Worcester Telegram & Gazette*

Growing up, my father was very focused on making sure that I was educated, and that I understood where I came from. In addition to regular school I went to Greek school, where I learned the language and other aspects of our culture. I was 14 years old in 1949 when I traveled to Greece with my father. It was exciting because nobody had gone to Greece much after the war. We went to the village where he was raised and there was a big family gathering. It was very emotional, and there were many tears of joy. His mother was still alive, and he saw siblings and cousins he hadn't seen since he was in his teens.

—JOANNA TSANDIKOS

A PILGRIMAGE FOR GEORGE

In 1949, George finally journeyed back to Greece. It was his first trip home in over three decades, and it was an understandably emotional reunion with his extended family. My mother, Joanna, was his traveling companion. It was not the only time George returned to Greece, but the first time back since he had left. It was the first of three trips.

George with his brother on his first visit back to Greece, c. 1949.

George was head of the Building Fund Committee for the new St. Spyridon Church that opened in 1952.

A Pillar of the Community

After World War II ended, Coney Island flourished and George finally achieved the financial prosperity he had been working so hard to attain since arriving in this country. It had been over 30 years since my grandfather had said goodbye to his village in Greece, yet in some ways he had never left the old country. He remained an integral part of Worcester's Greek community, and he was as driven and passionate in his commitment to St. Spyridon's Greek Orthodox Church as he was to his restaurant and family.

Being active in the Church was my grandfather's way of honoring his homeland and giving back to the community that had supported him as a young immigrant; his devotion to the Church was equaled only by his passionate commitment to Coney Island and his family. In 1944, George began serving as treasurer of a building fund committee dedicated to raising capitol for a new church to serve the steadily growing Greek community.

And, once the new church was built at the corner of Russell and Elm Streets, George remained a dedicated parishioner, even stopping by to water the lawn in the wee hours of the morning during times of drought—after incredibly long days working at Coney Island. George was eventually honored with the title of "Archon," one of the highest positions a lay person can hold in the Greek church.

Greek Archbishop to Give Liturgy

Archbishop Ezekiel, archbishop of the G r e e k Orthodox Church of Australia and New Zealand, shown with his host, George J. Tsagarelis of 17 Dorset St., will present the liturgy at 10 a.m. Sunday in St. Spyridon Greek Orthodox Church. He will be assisted by Rev. Arthur J. Rizos, pastor. Archbishop Ezekiel, former bishop of the New England Diocese of the Greek Orthodox Church, will preach the sermon at the conclusion of the liturgy. The archbishop is stopping in the United States on his way back to New Zealand and Australia, after visiting Greece.

Today, our family continues George's legacy not only through Coney Island, but through our involvement in the Church. My father, Fr. Solon Tsandikos, was a Greek Orthodox priest who served at St. Spyridon, and my brother, George Tsandikos, is an Archon in New York City.

(Left) The Archbishop of the Greek Orthodox Church of New Zealand and Australia presented the liturgy at the new St. Spyridon on Russell Street.
From the *Worcester Telegram & Gazette*

(Below) A church hierarch on a tour of the new church with George and members of the building committee.

Part 3
TRANSITIONS

In 1964, I was a member of the Notables Drum and Bugle Corps from Auburn. We played at the corner of Southbridge Street and Chandler Street as Lyndon Johnson drove from the airport to Holy Cross to deliver the commencement speech. So at least one sitting U.S. President has driven by Coney Island.

Years later, while attending college on the G.I. Bill, I was pretty poor. Loew's Poli movie theater, now the Hanover Theatre, was a couple of blocks down Southbridge Street from Coney Island. They had a special price for Saturday matinees. It was one dollar. My girlfriend, now my wife, and I would go over to Coney Island, buy a half dozen and eat them while watching the movie. The aroma would permeate the theater. I guarantee that as soon as the movie ended, everyone in that theater ran over to Coney Island.

—MICHAEL S. PROSTAK, B. 1948

(Above) President Lyndon Johnson's motorcade in Worcester, June 10, 1964.
From the collections of Worcester Historical Museum
(Opposite page) Photo by Ned McConnell

After cashing in two-cent and five-cent soda bottles, we went out. We bought a ten-cent bag of popcorn at Newberry's. Then we walked down Front Street to the family theater. At the time, a 14-cent ticket got you two features and four cartoons. The highlight of the day was a trip to Coney Island for hot dogs at ten cents each. When I was a sophomore at Commerce High School, I worked at a family grocery store, Poutre's Market on the corner of Madison Street and Salem Street. All of the neighborhood houses on Orange and Salem have been torn down and the families scattered. On Friday night and Saturday lunch, I would drink a bottle of milk with my hot dogs. After I got married and moved to Millbury and then Sutton, we would take our two daughters to Coney Island for a "special treat." Now I live in Texas, and when I visit my daughter, we always make a pilgrimage to the best damn hot dog place on God's green earth! Thank you for the memories!

—Ron Lemay, b. 1935

(Top) Downtown Worcester, 1962.

(Bottom) Denholms department store logo.

A Walking, Shopping, Thriving City

When my grandmother Catherine finished work at Coney Island in the afternoons, she'd take me with her to run errands. Occasionally, she even let me pick out something at Capitol Toy.

Thanks to the continued post-war economic boom that had recharged the city, Worcester was thriving during my childhood, and the neighborhood around Coney Island was bustling. In the 50s there was a barber shop on the corner of Southbridge Street as well as two other restaurants and a few bars nearby. There was also a clothing store next door, a shoe store, a rod and gun shop, and Worcester Rim & Wheel on another corner. Northridge Furniture, which took up a whole block, had apartments upstairs.

People from neighborhoods around Worcester would take the bus or walk downtown, especially on Saturdays and Wednesday nights, when the stores on Main Street stayed open late. Main Street was crowded with shoppers at those times and most dressed up for the occasion. Many headed for Filene's Basement, where you'd descend the stairs and see bargains piled high on tables, or for more sophisticated stores like Denholms, which offered spectacular window

Three generations of the Tsagarelis family on a visit to Greece, 1967. (Rear, left to right) Catherine and George Tsagarelis, Solon and Joanna Tsandikos. (Front) Kathryn, Stephanie, and George Tsandikos with Solon's Aunt Zoitsa.

We used to go to the movies at the Palace Theater at that time—then it was the Loew's Poli and now the Hanover Theater. After the movie, we would walk to Southbridge Street to Coney Island. As we got married in our twenties and had children, it was always a great experience to take the children there. Then, in our next step of life, we did square dancing. Late at night when square dancing was over, they were always open late, so our group would all go there for the end of our evening. There was always a crowd there when you went. Thanks for the memories!

—JOANN LEE, B. 1934

(Right) The former Loew's Poli Theater was restored and reopened in 2008 as the Hanover Theater.

displays and an elevator with a white-gloved operator who would call out each floor as the doors opened.

There was a Kresge's on Main Street and a Woolworths on Front Street, both popular with kids after school and families. A bounty of other stores and shops thrived downtown as well: Barnard's, Kennedy's, Marcus, Casual Corner, Diamond Jewelers, Regal Shoes, Whalen Jewelers, Bell Shops, Lerner's, and C.C. Lowell, the country's oldest art supplies store, which is still thriving to this day in its new location on Pleasant Street. There were bars and restaurants, and bowling alleys, and pool halls, too. Or you could go ice skating at Elm Park or see a concert. At Christmas, the entire city was lit up and you could hear music being piped from the various storefronts. Many people drove to the city from the surrounding towns simply to see the Christmas lights.

Whatever time of year it was, after they were done banking, shopping, and playing, people often found their way to Coney Island. College students and soldiers, families and boys on bikes, couples in love and older people who had found Coney Island when they were kids all came in to see us. Everyone was welcome, and we were always happy to put smiles on their faces, just as we are today.

On occasion, my buddies and I would come to Worcester by bus from Oxford to go to the movies (Loew's Poli, now Hanover Theatre). We always came to Coney Island after the movies. My name is on the wall in one of the booths. "Mike 1953"—I'd never find it now. I joined the Marine Corps in July 1954 and every time I came home on leave, a Coney Island stop was a necessity. I remember Brockelman's Market. It was up on the corner of Main Street where the unemployment office used to be. I stopped in Thursday, January 10, 2013. The hot dogs are still great. Coney Island was a legend in 1953 and still is. Keep up the tradition and keep them dogs a comin'.

—Edward W. Mickelson, b. 1937

I remember coming to Coney Island when I was seven years old. Up to the age of 13, I lived on Arwick Avenue, next to Nissen's Bakery. My mother and I would walk "downtown" to go shopping by way of Quinsigamond Avenue and Southbridge Street and often stop for lunch. On my 50th birthday, a milestone so to speak, I asked my family to take me out to eat at Coney Island. I was having lunch when the Northridge furniture store burned.

—Francis S. Ziarko, b. 1942

When I was six, Southbridge Street had a pet store. Farther up there was a public market. Barr's Shoe was on the corner. We walked everywhere and lived on Orange Street. I would come with my aunt and uncle. She would eat the bun and sauce. I ate the hot dog.

—Naomi Hartigan Nichols, b. 1942

Returning from the movies in the 1950s, we would stop and look in the window at the hundreds of franks on the grill. One of the senior cooks would call us in and give us the broken franks for free, which we enjoyed for the walk back to Cambridge Street near St. John's cemetery, now fueled by Coney Island hot dogs given to the two of us.

—Ed, b. 1943

I remember coming to Coney Island when I was ten years old. No downtown and no mall now! Maybe we will have a downtown again. After my grandsons played basketball at the Y, we would come for lunch every week. When my brothers come from California and Connecticut, they always have to come to Coney Island for the BEST HOT DOGS.

—Pamela Kazarian, b. 1944

When I was six years old, I would come to Worcester to shop at Denholms and Filene's with my sister and mom. It was our tradition to stop every time we would go to the "big city to get ready for school." I would always have three hot dogs.

—Paula Chauvin, b. 1945

On Saturday, we would go to the movies. Then my mother would window shop at the Northridge Furniture store. Then we'd come in and have two hot dogs for 15 cents and chocolate milk for 10 cents. My favorite memory is of watching the employees line up 10 or 12 hot dogs on their arms, putting on the mustard, sauce, and onions.

—Earl LeBel, b. 1946

I come from a family of eight children. Our parents would take us to the Mart, then to Barr's Shoes, then here for hot dogs. My husband and I were married 46 years ago in November. We also brought our children and grandchildren here when we would come to Worcester to see a movie. When we were dating in the 1960s, we would come here after or before the Holy Cross basketball games. He and his family always come here after Holy Cross football games. My dad will soon be 98 years old. This is where he wants to come for a hot dog after his doctor's appointments. Sometimes the only way we can get him to his appointments is to tell him we will get a hot dog after.

—Shirley Splaine, b. 1947

Every Saturday, my father (Raymond J. Alukas) and I would load up the trunk with yard waste and trash, go to the dump, and always stop at Coney Island for three dogs "up" each and a chocolate milk (my father had a beer). He told me this was our secret and not to tell my mom. Loved it then, love it now. My dad passed away January 7, 2012. He was 91.

—Patricia Louise (Alukas) Kleinman

I grew up on Pakachoag Hill. For years before I-290, we went downtown via Southbridge Street. That meant going by Coney Island twice. Back then, they served Weigert hot dogs made right here in Worcester. They bought them in a roll like a hose and cut them to length so the ends were square, not domed like today. The chocolate milk came in glass bottles shaped like a milk can and served with a paper straw. The rolls, chili sauce, mustard, and onions are all pretty much the same. The building is also very much the same. New outside doors and unfortunately a new jukebox.

—Michael S. Prostak

I've been coming to Coney Island for over 60 years. I grew up in Worcester from 1943 to 1965. That's when we moved to New Hampshire. I first came to Coney Island because I would go to the Musical Café next door. The Musical Café in the early 1950s was an underground gay bar, which attracted both gay men and lesbians. Many times I was arrested at the Musical Café, but sometimes we would come next door to Coney Island where we'd be safe from arrest. Coney Island was a sanctuary for us! I don't know where the gay bars are anymore. But today we don't need them, because we're open and free!

—Lynn Berry

There was a lot of turmoil in Coney Island back in the 1950s. We served a lot of soldiers because Worcester was the nearest big city for those on furlough from Fort Devens. George had to hire policemen on Saturday nights because the bars used to close at two o'clock or something. On one occasion, a fight started outside the restaurant, so one of the workers asked the policeman if he was going to break it up. He replied, "Oh, just let them fight." George didn't like that. He fired the policeman and took over keeping the peace. And I'll tell you, there were no fights or any funny business after that.

—FR. SOLON TSANDIKOS
GEORGE AND CATHERINE'S SON-IN-LAW

The secret sauce.
Photo by Mike Henderickson

I remember coming to Coney Island when I was three years old. A couple of families would go to the airport to watch the planes at night. Then we would come here. That was always the exciting part.

—MARTHA HOGAN OLSON, B. 1950

During the 1960s, my dad would take us frequently to the new library at Salem Square. Though I remember the Elm Street one! After the library, we headed down to Coney Island. To get us to eat the hot dogs with chili, he told us it was called "mystery sauce." I am still enjoying two "up" with mystery sauce, even today, as are my own children. When pregnant with my second son, I craved Coney Island hot dogs and came every Thursday with my one-and-a-half-year-old son after swimming at the YMCA. One Tuesday night, my husband drove down to Coney Island to satisfy my craving. To this day, I know you are closed on Tuesday. Thank you for great hot dogs and for keeping this Worcester tradition alive!

—ANNIE DOLAN, B. 1955

I remember coming to Coney Island after roller skating at Mechanics Hall when I was 12 years old. We would play three songs on the jukebox for 25 cents.

—DEB, B. 1959

My mom and dad used to take my older brother, my younger brother and me to Coney Island every Saturday after baths. From there we'd go to White City, the amusement park. Later on, I went a lot of times with my husband Don. I've taken my kids as a treat—then we'd go get ice cream. It's funny that now my children go themselves. They carry on the tradition.

—RUTH ROY

I remember coming to Coney Island when I was 11 years old. I took keyboard lessons at Union Music next door. My mom, Elaine Ballon, always brought me over for hot dogs and chocolate milk afterward. I still come often. My order is four with sauce and two chocolate milks.

—LUCAS BALLON, AKA LUKE BASS, B. 1975

From the age of three, my dad and I would visit the Worcester Public Library and then get Coney Island dogs (mine just with ketchup) after school, about twice a month. I used to always play a Steely Dan song on the jukebox when I got older. I still get my dogs with cream soda every time.

—KATIE MCCARTHY, B. 1984

WEATHERING ANOTHER TOUGH TRANSITION

In the 1970s, Worcester began experiencing yet another transition. It wasn't an easy one for the city and its people, or for Coney Island either.

It's difficult to pinpoint exactly when the decline began, but as manufacturing changed, there was less demand for goods. Factories were becoming more automated too, and needed fewer workers. That decline in jobs took a heavy toll on the working community, especially on immigrants like my grandfather who had come to this part of the world seeking better opportunities.

Without the war bringing soldiers to Fort Devens, they stopped arriving in Worcester by the trainload as they had before. And, as business began going global, companies were moving much of their manufacturing abroad to take advantage of cheaper unskilled labor forces.

In Worcester, too, there was a change in the city meant to make life easier for commuters, but one that ended up having a negative impact on the formerly bustling downtown: the construction of Interstate 290, a 20-mile stretch of highway winding along the southern edge of Worcester and connecting Auburn and Marlborough. The construction itself was a major disruption, lasting from 1958 throughout the 1960s, but even worse was the fact that the city was now bisected and less walkable. People began moving into suburbs north or west of the city, and at times downtown Worcester felt like a ghost town.

In an attempt to revitalize the area, city developers approved the demolition of a large swath of downtown to make room for the construction of Worcester Center Galleria in 1971. The two-story

(Above) Parts of the city center were demolished to make way for the Galleria and Worcester Centrum.
From the collections of Worcester Historical Museum

I-290 went in, and many of the Greek families from the east side moved to the west side. Our original church, St. Spyridon's on Orange Street, was torn down. Worcester was no longer a walking city, and the Southbridge Street neighborhood slowly began to lose one business after another. Our customers no longer walked to Coney Island, most of them came by car. Worcester was an example of urban renewal gone bad. It divided the city.

—Joanna Tsandikos

• • • • • • • • • • • • • •

shopping mall remained open for the next two decades, effectively forcing the closure of remaining small retail businesses in Worcester and continuing the city's transition to a car-friendly destination rather than a walkable city. Ultimately, the Worcester Center Galleria failed to attract enough customers from its suburban competitors, like the Auburn Mall and the Greendale Mall, and it closed, too.

Every generation comes with the good and the bad, with advantages and hardships. Thankfully, Worcester is resilient. Many of its residents are firmly rooted here, thanks to great-grandparents and grandparents who saw their opportunities in this city and made lives for themselves, as my grandfather did. Immigrants continued to arrive, newcomers striving to work hard and make the world a better place for themselves, their families back home, and their children.

And Coney Island stayed open throughout this economic downturn, doing what we do best: giving people opportunities to come together and make memories.

(Below) Customers waiting in line to order.
Photo by Dany Pelletier

The mural that spans the back of the restaurant was refurbished in the 1980s and featured in the 1999 *Worcester Scenes* calendar.
Photo by Brian Fallon Crowley

THE MURAL

Always the entrepreneur, George realized that the back of the building provided the perfect advertising opportunity. Why not put up a billboard for all of those city drivers who would be passing by?

And so a mural was born. The original artist, whose name is lost to history, laid down a bright yellow backdrop on the red brick exterior and rec-reated Romanov's rendition of George's hand holding a hot dog dripping with mustard. Passersby to the south of the restaurant now had a beacon to beckon them in for a Coney dog. The mural was refurbished in the mid-1980s. It remains a part of the exterior décor to this day—unchanged, just the way our customers like things.

(Below) The mural before its face lift.

Worcester continues to experience transformations. Today, that ghost town of the 1970s is an exciting draw for businesses, artists, restaurant owners, college students, and families. You can go to a concert at the DCU Center, the Palladium, or Mechanics Hall, or see a musical at the Hanover Theatre, then walk to a bar or a restaurant. You can even play ice hockey or go figure skating at the Fidelity Bank Worcester Ice Center. As this book goes to press, the new Polar Park is getting ready to host the WooSox.

In the Canal District, restaurants and bars seem to be popping up by the week. Shrewsbury Street is once again Restaurant Row. Colleges have opened campuses downtown, like the Massachusetts College of Pharmacy and Health Sciences campus and WPI's Life Sciences and Bioengineering Center.

Worcester is welcoming new start-ups and bio-tech companies. Meanwhile, the $565 million City Square project has razed the former Worcester Center Galleria/Worcester Common Fashion Outlets to reopen Front Street. This means that Worcester's downtown is once again connected to Washington Square, Shrewsbury Street, and the Canal District.

The demographics of the city's immigrants have changed from Irish and Greek to Latin American, African, and Vietnamese. People are still coming to Worcester from around the world for better work and educational opportunities. With every passing generation, Worcester's immigrants have continued to enrich our city's cultural identity.

As Worcester has undergone changes, so has Coney Island. Instead of serving working people and a big nighttime crowd who arrive on foot, by bus, or by bicycle, we are now mostly serving shoppers, commuters, college students, and families who come by car.

But the more things change, the more Coney Island stays the same. We are intent on delivering affordable quality food, and to providing a haven for hot dog lovers. Our family has kept Coney Island true to its roots partly by keeping the business right in the family, passing the torch (and the recipe for that secret sauce) down through the generations.

● ● ● ● ● ● ● ● ● ● ● ● ● ● ● ● ● ● ● ●

I've been coming to Coney Island since I was a little boy in the 1970s. Our son, Adam, plays basketball at Friendly House on Saturdays, then we come here for a treat. Also, Coney Island is our favorite summer stop. We've watched Worcester transform from a manufacturing city to a combination of biotech and software-based economy. Over the years, Worcester has become diversified in culture and has grown dramatically in population.

—Chris DesRosiers

Worcester's historic Town Hall with the World War II monument in the foreground. Photo by Dany Pelletier

SAYING SAD BUT PROUD GOODBYES

George J. Tsagarelis, Owner Of Coney Island Restaurant

George J. Tsagarelis, 80, of 17 Dorset St., owner of George's Coney Island Restaurant, 158 Southbridge St., for 51 years, died yesterday in City Hospital.

Mr. Tsagarelis was president of St. Spyridon Greek Orthodox Church, 102 Russell St., at the time it was built and consecrated in 1952.

He leaves his wife, Catherine (Angelopoulos) Tsagarelis; a daughter, Joanna A., wife of the Rev. Solon Tsandikos of Paxton; two sisters, Angelike Rassias of Worcester, and Helen Pappas of Athens, Greece; a grandson, George Tsandikos, and two granddaughters, Kathryn and Stephanie Tsandikos, all of Paxton.

Born in Pikerni, Arcadia, Greece, he was a son of John T. and Demetria (Pappas) Tsagarelis, and moved to Worcester from Haverhill 60 years ago. He came to the United States at the age of 17 and lived in Haverhill eight years.

He had been a member of the Order of AHEPA 40 years, and was a member of the board of trustees of Holy Cross Greek Orthodox Theological Seminary, Brookline, and the Archdiocesan Council of the Greek Orthodox Church of North and South America.

The Ecumenical Patriarch of Constantinople conferred the title of archon on him in recognition of his philanthropic and personal services to the church as a layman.

During World War II, he was a member of the Greek War Relief Committee. In 1961 the Ladies Philoptohos Society of St. Spyridon gave him its Man of the Year Award.

Mr. Tsagarelis had been treasurer of his church's building fund committee 17 years.

Funeral services will be at 11 a.m. Wednesday in St. Spyridon Greek Orthodox Church, 102 Russell St. Archbishop Iakovos of Boston will officiate.

Burial will be in Hope Cemetery.

Mr. Tsagarelis

Calling hours at the church are 3 to 9 p.m. tomorrow.

The family requests flowers be omitted. Memorial contributions may be made instead to Holy Cross Greek Orthodox Theological Seminary, 50 Goddard St., Brookline.

O'Connor Brothers, 592 Park Ave., is directing arrangements.

As he entered his seventies, my grandfather began spending less time in the restaurant that bore his name. George passed away in 1980 at the age of eighty. He created a great legacy in the form of a business that not only continues to sustain our family, but serves as an iconic treasure providing generations of families with good food and cherished memories.

Beginning in the early to mid-1970s, my grandmother ran nearly every aspect of the business. She had always been a formidable half of their duo, and she had been doing the ordering and keeping the books, among other essential tasks. Catherine made sure that Coney Island continued serving loyal customers, old and new, and she still loved telling stories—almost as much as she loved listening to our customers tell theirs.

(Left) Obituary of George Tsagarelis in the *Worcester Telegram & Gazette.*

(Below) George with granddaughter Kathryn.

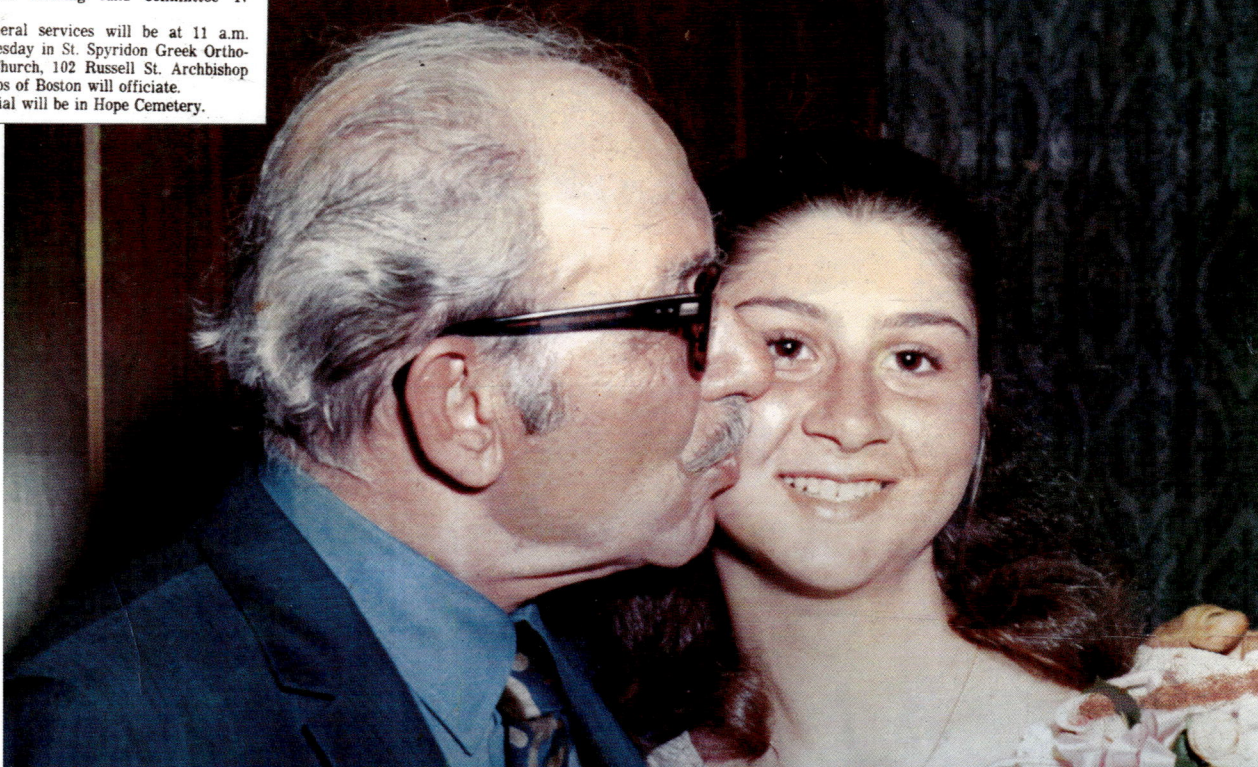

I didn't know George, but I did have a chance to know my grandmother, Catherine. I knew her as a very funny person. I think it's a special kind of person who can talk with a kid and make them feel like an adult, or make them feel like they're an actual person. I think she probably learned this from being in the restaurant business and interacting with so many people. She had a real sense of humor. I remember I asked her if she still had her real teeth. She didn't even answer me. She just took her dentures out right there.

—SOLON KELLEHER
GEORGE & CATHERINE'S GREAT-GRANDSON

Catherine continued working full-time at Coney Island until she suffered a stroke in 1992. After that, she had to slow down a bit, but even into her eighties she would stay late to share a glass of beer with the young men who closed the restaurant. People still remember her fondly—her love of life, her stories, her kindness, her laugh—and her Cadillacs. I think of her every day and believe she's watching over us.

Catherine was a sweetheart. After many moons I returned to Worcester. I had to stop in at Coney Island. I couldn't believe how much Kathryn looks like her grandmother.

—LARRY GRIZZLY FLEMING

(Top) Catherine Tsagarelis with Kathryn and great-grandchildren.

(Bottom) The funeral procession of Catherine Tsagarelis paused in front of the restaurant, 1992.
From the *Worcester Telegram & Gazette*

77

His Counseling Is Side Order At Restaurant In Worcester

By Rachel Lahti DeFuria
Of the Regional Staff

CLINTON — A disturbing aspect of being a member of the clergy is that "we must have an answer to everything in life. All of a sudden we have got to have answers for all the problems that confront the United Nations," says the Rev. Dr. Solon S. Tsandikos.

"I am not that wise. I am constantly seeking, asking, wondering, doubting," says the 53-year-old pastor of St. Nicholas Greek Orthodox Church, who was ordained a priest 25 years ago.

"For a moment I may even doubt my own purpose. It's a disturbing thing ... but man must keep on searching and seeking. If we ever stop searching and seeking, that's when we must be afraid," he said.

"God is around us, but we are blind to him most of the time," he said.

"If I tell you to look at the stars or go in the woods, we are too blind to touch him there. I think we have to reach within ourselves to find him, but to reach within ourselves, we need that word of God (the Bible) ... " Father Tsandikos said.

"As I grow older, I find I believe more in God, and I keep striving to believe more in God. I try to get away from needing too much and try to live more simply ... The more I believe in him, the more free I get from these things ...

"I must learn to live this moment as if the next one will be the last one of my life," he said. Life should be lived to the fullest. A waste of life is something awful, he said.

Tries to Be Alone

When he has a problem and is searching for an answer, he goes someplace where he is alone. "Somehow it's a form of prayer, and I will contemplate. Sometimes it's very very tiring and exhausting," he said.

The Rev. Dr. Solon S. Tsandikos

"An awful lot of people come here (George's Coney Island Lunch on Southbridge Street) to talk to me. I have done more counseling here than in a parish. Some are people I have never seen before and probably will never see again. They come just for counseling. Somehow they found I am down here, and they want to talk to someone,"

The Rev. Dr. Solon S. Tsandikos

(Above) Fr. Solon Tsandikos, George and Catherine's son-in-law, ministered to many Coney Island patrons.

(Below) With Governor Deval Patrick.

New Faces Behind the Counter

Fortunately, by the time George was ready to leave Coney Island, my father, Fr. Solon Tsandikos, was already stepping in to fill the void and help Catherine manage the business. Born in Lowell, Massachusetts, to Anthe and Stephanos Tsandikos, my father graduated from Holy Cross Seminary in Brookline in 1953 before entering Andover Newton Theological School, where he received his bachelor of divinity degree in 1955. He married my mother that same year, then earned a master's degree in social theology.

After a trip to Greece, where my father earned his theology doctorate at the University of Athens, he served at three Massachusetts churches: Holy Trinity in Fitchburg, St. Spyridon in Worcester, and Saint Nicholas in Clinton. In addition to his parish ministry, my father was a pioneer in the ecumenical movement and was a founding member of the first Interfaith Council in Worcester. He has also served as a trustee of Hellenic College/Holy

A caricature of Fr. Solon.

I remember coming to Coney Island when I was four years old. I remember coming here with my dad and meeting Reverend Solon. He married my parents in 1991.

—ARISTIDIS NATSIS, B. 1993

Fr. Solon with his grandchildren.

Cross Seminary and on the Spiritual Council of Orthodox Churches in the New England Diocese, among other things.

Most important of all, my father brought his caring, generous heart and profound spirituality to Coney Island as he entered the family business to take some of the burden off my grandmother's shoulders. Just like George and Catherine before him, Fr. Solon became a friendly, familiar face to our loyal customers and was one of my most important role models. Not many daughters have the opportunity to work alongside their fathers, and I'm so proud to be one of those lucky few.

For the customers who were aware of my dad's dual role as priest and restaurateur, Fr. Solon offered more than just a good meal at a fair price. He had headed parishes in Fitchburg and Worcester for a combined 16 years before taking on the smaller parish in Clinton and donning an apron to serve our customers at Coney Island, so it was only natural for people to confide in him and ask for advice.

"An awful lot of people come here to talk to me," Dad said. "I have done more counseling than in a parish. Some are people I have never seen before and probably will never see again. They come here just for counseling. Somehow they found I am down here, and they want to talk to someone."

For many, Fr. Solon embodied the family aspect of George's Coney Island. He emphasized that as he gradually reduced our evening hours and began promoting Coney Island as a friendly family eatery rather than a night spot.

I loved watching my father give people his full attention and listen to them. No matter how much work he had to do, my father took his counseling role seriously. While food may feed our bodies, the ritual of dining and talking together feeds our souls, and my father knew this better than anyone. He became the heart of Coney Island after my grandparents were gone, and being able to work with him and witness his kindness and compassion toward others was a tremendous gift.

My mother, Joanna, sometimes regretted not having been more involved with the business, but like most new immigrants, her father was adamant that she had a better life than he'd had—one where she would go to college and not have to work as hard as my grandparents.

Still, my mother spent much of her childhood at Coney Island, absorbing business sense and a valuable work ethic. After attending Mt. Ida College, she worked hard to keep an elegant home and raise my brother, sister, and me to do well in school and work as hard as the rest of the family—all while serving the Greek community in her role as a priest's wife.

For my parents, seeing their children become educated, responsible adults eager to serve others was of paramount importance, and they succeeded: I graduated from Boston College, my brother graduated from Brown University and Boston College School of Law, and my sister earned her undergraduate degree at Smith College and her doctorate in psychology at Fordham University. We absorbed the work ethic of our parents and grandparents and set out to make the world a better place.

Gradually, I assumed the reins at Coney Island from my father, and I am so honored to be carrying on our family's legacy. I hope one day to pass that legacy on to my own two children, Solon and Alexis, who has already opened Crust, a bakery of her own in Worcester.

Joanna Tsandikos behind the counter.
From *Yankee* magazine, 1985

I remember coming to Coney Island when I was 15 years old. When I was skinnier, I would order four "up!" I remember bringing my daughters here for the first time to carry on the tradition.

—CARL RAPP, B. 1960

(Left) Joanna with Catherine, c. 1990.

(Opposite page) Kathryn carries on the family tradition.

Telegram Staff Photo by BILL BARRY

ON THE DOG. In 41 years George J. Tsagarelis has sold 120 tons of his
nd babies.

With a few tons of mustard on the side

Coney Island today can handle 250 people, either in booths or at the counters, a far cry from the early days.

Talking about the old days, George described how he purchased hot dogs in 30- or 40-foot strips. He cut them 12 to a pound. He stopped doing that a couple of years ago — "It's easier to buy them all cut," he confessed.

"In those days," he added, "we used to sell to hospitals, schools and the jail." That has now been done away with, and for the same reason — "Too much trouble, too busy."

When he started in business the hot dog sold for 5 cents. Today, with all the trimmings, he sells it for a quarter. And he can proudly point out that he has been serving four and five generations of some families.

"Business is just as good as it was years ago," he is quick to tell you. He has had many orders for as much as 40 hot dogs — and a million for just one.

"The cash intake is higher — but so is the cost of the frankfurts, rolls, relish, and onions," he points out.

He has constantly improved the fixtures, added one of the best air-conditioning units available a few years ago, and is "certain" his outlet is as good as any similar operation in the country.

He has a good word for his customers, those who have been coming for years as well as the younger generation.

"There is nothing wrong with the youngsters," he emphasizes, adding, "they all behave well."

And as he left us to serve another customer, he remarked, "they had better behave — or else." □

(John Cronin conducts the popular

By John T. Cronin

THE HOT DOG was supposedly made famous at Coney Island, N.Y.

Well, it could have been.

But, there's no doubt at all that George J. Tsagarelis of 17 Dorset St., who operates Coney Island on Southbridge Street, sure made it famous in these parts.

And he has the figures to prove it.

George, who purchased the business back in 1929, can show you that from 1929 to 1969, he sold 120 tons of hot dogs, used 36 tons of sauce, 480 tons of onions, 9,600 gallons of mustard and close to 3 million rolls.

bridge Street — a small counter-and-nine-stool lunchroom, adjacent to the building he has now occupied for many years.

He brought along one counterman, a George O'Neil, who had worked with him at the Alpha.

They worked 12 hours a day, seven days a week in building up the business.

Evidently they had the secret. There were five other similar establishments on Southbridge Street, between Madison to Herman streets. They all went out of business within a few years.

Today, George employs 18 people. One of them, Paul Minka, an assistant manager, has been with him for

Part 4
CONEY ISLAND MEMORIES

I remember coming to Coney Island when I was five years old. My mother was a single mother. She used to take us to the ocean in Rhode Island on Sundays, and we would stop here for hot dogs before we went on our weekend trips in the summer. I used to come here as a teenager, too. I introduced my friends to this place. They loved it, and we would come here for hot dogs and to hang out. I now come here with my 11-year-old son as our special place, just me and him, when I want to get away. We even have our own booth. When I was pregnant, I lived in Oklahoma and I craved Coney Island. A good friend of mine used to send me bags with the smell of Coney Island to help curb the cravings. I was so appreciative. It was a taste of home and a sense of comfort.

—Stephanie Williams, b. 1981

Christo Vrusho worked at Coney for over 50 years.

Counterman Paul Wassel.

CONEY ISLAND EMPLOYEES

Our employees have been every bit as important in creating and upholding the legacy of Coney Island as our customers. Many of them stay with us for decades and have become part of our extended family. Our employees exhibit a rare dedication, loyalty, and work ethic and truly make this place special. We know they will step in to help us, just as our employees can count on us being there to help them any way we can. Together, we create a unique sort of atmosphere, an environment where all of our customers—young or old, rich or poor, of any cultural background—know they can walk in and be treated with respect and kindness. That's why so many of our customers quickly feel like they're part of our extended family.

It takes a special sort of person to work at Coney Island, one who is fast, focused, patient, and polite—all while juggling several moving parts behind our narrow counter. I think of us as some complex organism, like an amoeba. All of us have to work together without constantly bumping into each other as we cook dogs and load them up with various condiments, and then pair them up with the right drinks and chips for the right customers, all while chatting with each other and making sure the faces behind the counter are smiling.

I remember coming to Coney Island when I was seven years old. My uncle, Paul Wassel, worked here, and we would ask for the sauce recipe. He would always tell us "next time," but we never did get it. He took it to his grave with him. We used to come in groups to eat hot dogs until we got sick. I think one guy ate 13 in a half hour. That was in the early 70s. Yes, he had the munchies.

—ED RIVERS, B. 1955

(Left to right) Bukurije Paloja, Cedric Nsilo-Swai, Eric-John Yankus Franco, Hieu Huynh, Will Jacobsen.

Staff at Coney Island's 100th anniversary party, 2018. Eric-John Yankus Franco, Therese Totolas, Josh Holden, Ginger Rabine, Ida Treska, Bukurije Paloja, Jorge Cruz, Kevin Oliver, Brendan Vargeletis, Will Jacobsen, Mett Shala.

George's Coney Island Hot Dog is an oasis of unchanging history in our ever-changing culture.

—Blu Shihko

I remember coming to Coney Island when I was five years old. I have so many memories. My dad, Armand Towers, was a fixture here. He worked at Northridge Furniture Company next door. Coney Island was our family place. Catherine and George were always icons to us. I remember Paul and Chris behind the counter with eight to ten dogs on one arm and filling them with our order, mainly "the works." Some things change, but even today I still come here for those hot dogs and chocolate milk (still remain the best dogs ever).

—Dottie Harlow, b. 1945

I used to clean the tables when my dad, Vangel, chopped onions in the back room. Now I come here with my grandchildren.

—Barbara Grady, b. 1950

My father, Chris Vrusho (see photo opposite page), started working at Coney Island right after World War II. He worked there for 52 years! I grew up hanging around the place. I would sit with Roger, one of the workers, in the back room, peeling onions. They brought their rolls from the Town Talk bakery, the only ones who sold the two-sided hot dog roll they used. I remember my dad taking a cab to Town Talk in an emergency run to get more rolls when we ran out.

—Bob Vrusho

The people that work there go a hundred miles an hour, move through hundreds of people in minutes, and still remain friendly and helpful. That's why they do such a good business, and that's why everything is so fresh and good.

—Bob Nordstrom

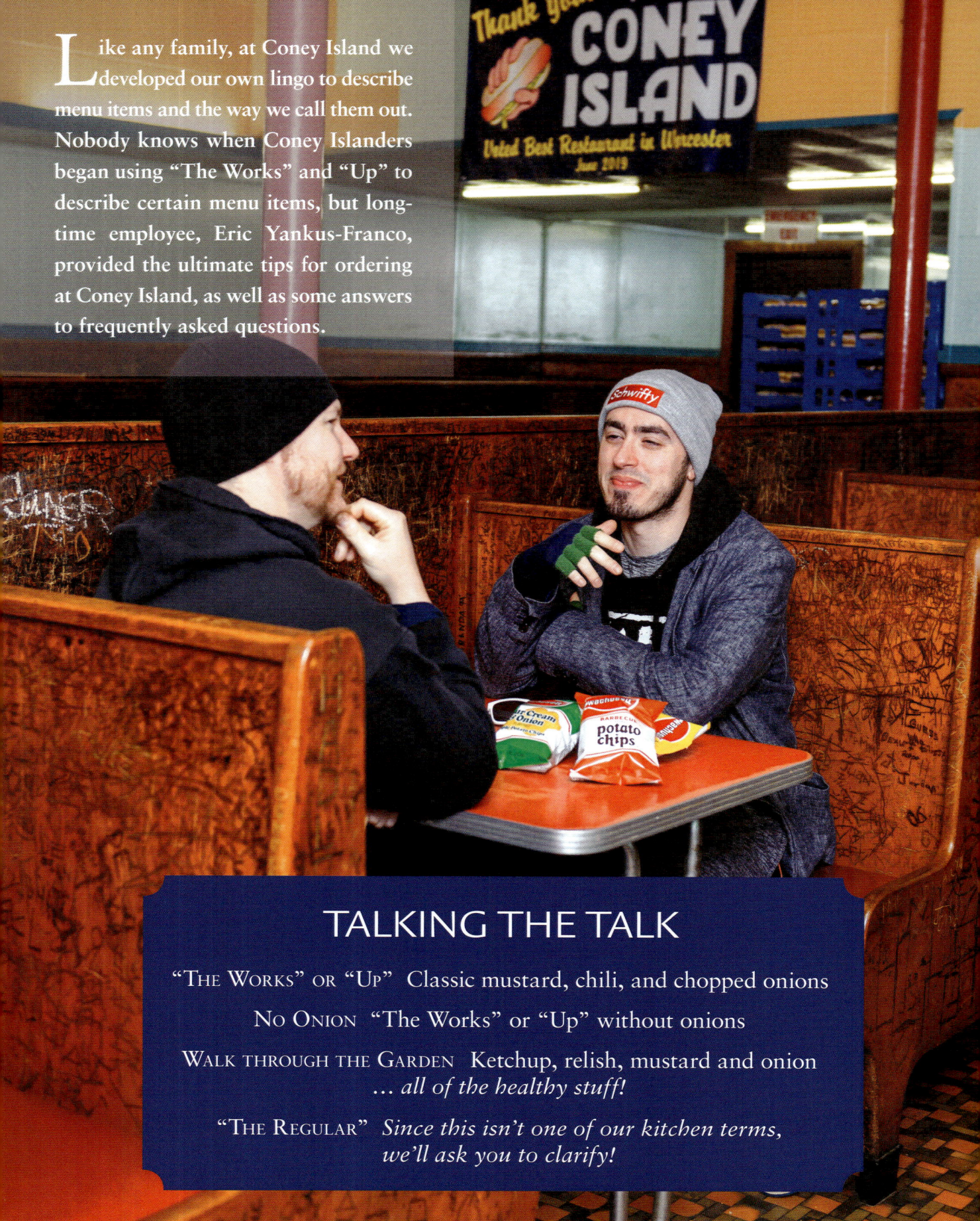

Like any family, at Coney Island we developed our own lingo to describe menu items and the way we call them out. Nobody knows when Coney Islanders began using "The Works" and "Up" to describe certain menu items, but long-time employee, Eric Yankus-Franco, provided the ultimate tips for ordering at Coney Island, as well as some answers to frequently asked questions.

TALKING THE TALK

"THE WORKS" OR "UP" Classic mustard, chili, and chopped onions

NO ONION "The Works" or "Up" without onions

WALK THROUGH THE GARDEN Ketchup, relish, mustard and onion
… all of the healthy stuff!

"THE REGULAR" *Since this isn't one of our kitchen terms, we'll ask you to clarify!*

My grandfather brought my sister, brother and me here as a special treat. We were all so excited, since he had been telling us about Coney Island for a week. Now I'm bringing my own grandchildren here.

—DEBBIE DELISIO, B. 1950

We visited on many occasions with my children, and now my grandchildren. I was here to celebrate my first grandson's sixth birthday. When I was his age, my grandpa told me how he had installed the floor at Coney Island. Now I tell my grandson the same story. Coney Island is an institution. Never close!

—MIKE, B. 1957

(Opposite page) Rich Crowley and Vincent Cirigliano enjoying a late lunch. Photo by Dany Pelletier

FAMILY TRADITIONS

From special Saturday afternoon treats to birthday celebrations, from Christmas holidays to school vacations, some of our favorite stories are from people who first began coming to Coney Island with their parents and grandparents, and are now bringing their own children and grandkids to make memories over hot dogs as they listen to the jukebox.

(Above) The bar at Coney Island.
Photo by Habbakuk Media Services

As a lifelong Worcester resident, I can remember my initial indoctrination to Coney Island. In the summer of 1955, as a six-year-old boy staying with my grandparents at their home on Plantation Street, my grandfather, Nazarino Cunsi, who was a salesman, would come home at lunchtime and bring me to Coney Island for a hot dog and a chocolate milk! I always looked forward to that. Later on, I can remember how, at almost every large family gathering, my grandfather would disappear and show up later with several boxes of piping hot dogs! I carried on the tradition with my own family by making Coney Island a regular stop during our family time. To this day, I attend most of the Holy Cross athletic events and invariably make Coney Island hot dogs to be a part of my upbringing, and part of my roots, growing up and residing as an adult in Worcester.

—Peter J. Pats

I've been coming to Coney since the early 1960s, and I still eat here! I've lived in Millbury, MA, since 1952, the year I was born. My father was born in Millbury in 1913. My mother was born in Millbury in 1918. My brother was born in 1949. We always had wonderful memories of George's Coney Island. We ate here after shopping in downtown Worcester and after going to the cinema. On Saturdays the place was packed with people listening to the jukebox, which had 45 rpm records at the time. My aunt came in for lunch when she worked at Wyman-Gordon near here in the 1940s. My brother and I went to Holy Name High School when it was in the Main South area. It moved in 1967.

In the mid-1950s to mid-1960s, my mother would take my brother and me to downtown Worcester on the bus from Millbury. Newberry 5&10, Woolworth's, Denholm's, Kresge's, Grant's, and many more. Back then, a frappe was 50 cents. Men were dressed in hats and women wore dresses, nice shoes, and many had nice white gloves. In the early 1970s, the Worcester Galleria Mall opened and changed the landscape of downtown Worcester. Coney Island seemed to be the same: the building

facade, wooden seats and sides with graffiti carved in, and still the same delicious hot dogs.

Today, Coney Island still retains the charm of yesteryear, although the computer-type machine has replaced 45s. My mother, father, and aunt have passed away, but I still have memories of being here with them at Coney Island and having a good meal and a good time. The workers and service are still excellent here at this famous downtown eating place.

—Gary Dwinell, b. 1952

I remember coming to Coney Island when I was 40 years old. I have come here for dinner on special weekends with a special group of friends. We have always been welcomed with open arms, great service, and good food. It has been an important part of the weekends in my life. I hope Coney Island continues its strong tradition of excellence of execution, inclusiveness, "nonjudgmental-ness," and quality that has kept me coming back each year. Keep up the good work. I am the third generation of my family enjoying your great food and great atmosphere.

—Gregg Hutzhing, b. 1958

I've been coming to Coney for 50 years, since I was five years old. My mother and father used to bring us to listen to the jukebox while they had a pitcher of beer. We danced and had fun, but Dad wouldn't let me carve my name into the booth. Worcester has changed with time, but I love our city.

—Dory

Every Christmas season, our family of over 30 people would come here after a cold morning cutting down Christmas trees. One year, my brother-in-law ate 39 hot dogs! His name is Victor Ceccarini of Worcester. We came here for at least ten years straight! We will never forget Coney Island.

—Deborah Ceccarini, b. 1954

I remember coming to Coney Island when I was eight years old in 1957. Since I was a young girl, my father would bring me here to have a hot dog, chips, and a chocolate milk. He would always give me money to play the jukebox. We would come here after visiting the Woolworth's building, since we always wanted to see the pet area. Then we would travel over to the other part of Main Street to Manzi's Insurance Company, so my dad could visit and pay his bill. Our visits were mainly during school vacation week and I looked forward to this experience every vacation. Another thing we did was to visit Water Street for bulky rolls and pickled herring at Tom's Meat Market. Great times. I've carried on the family tradition: I started taking my two kids here at a young age. We always play the jukebox and have hot dogs, chips, and chocolate milk.

—Carol A. Fidrych-Duda, b. 1959

Thank you for the time at Coney Island on May 24th (2008) for my father's 80th birthday. It made his day! And thank you for the T-shirt, we may never get it off him. It was a memorable day, you're the best!

—Dave Gabree

When I was seven years old, I would try to eat as many hot dogs as my mother and three brothers. I never could, though. We used to fight over what songs to play on the jukebox. This was the first hot dog place we brought our daughters to, and they loved it so much, we never go anywhere else. Now, our tradition is always celebrating a big birthday with the family here at Coney.

—LINDA S. MEDEIROS, B. 1963

My family and I came here a lot when I was six. I remember always going over to the jukebox and playing a different song. Nothing has really changed except there's a new jukebox.

—REBECCA, B. 1998

My uncle took me here once when I was nine, but I was hooked at age 11. I would come here once a week. It was my favorite place then and it is still to this day. I have six children and this is their reward place. We come to our table—the one next to the jukebox. We play music and just talk. Now they know, when they are super, they get Coney Island.

—JAMES TRUDELL, JR., B. 1970

I've been coming to Coney Island since I was two years old. My brother and I loved hot dogs. The one thing I remember about my first time here is the jukebox.

—LIL NICK AND ARIANNA, B. 2003 AND 1998

I remember coming to Coney Island when I was six or seven years old. When I was little, I came in with my mom and grandma. They each had two hot dogs and I only had one, so I cried and cried. Finally, my mom grabbed my hot dog, broke it in half, and said, "There, now you have two." I stopped crying. I came here often, at least once per week.

—BOB BROWN, B. 1955

I remember when I was six years old, I came here with my parents and siblings. The hot dogs looked so big, ha ha. My mom would say all day to us that we were going somewhere special and it was a surprise until we got here! Yes, then my husband and I came here when we were dating. We carved our names on the wall (oops). Now, 14 years later, we come and look for it while we eat, but I can't find it. We still have memories. Thank you!

—LINDA RIVERA, B. 1961

No hot dog is better than a Coney hot dog! My great-grandparents and grandparents would bring me. Also, my dad, may he rest in peace, always would take the family to Coney. My dad, if he could have anything to eat, it would be a Coney dog. So from then on, I have always tried to bring my kids and family to carry on the tradition!

—JAMES COLAIZZI, B. 1967

My husband grew up in Worcester. We lived in Somers, CT, for 26 years before moving to Oregon in 1992. We came to Worcester often, and we never left town without a visit to Coney Island Hot Dogs. I always loved the place, especially because of the food, old-time atmosphere, and the family-owned aspect. We brought our children here, too.

—Vivian Duhart, b. 1943

So many fond memories of my whole family eating here together. Though the city has changed a lot since then, Coney Island remains the BEST hot dog around. Thank you for not changing the décor of Coney Island. Our sons and daughters, nieces and nephews can see Coney Island exactly as it's always been! Thank you for what you do here.

—Kevin, b. 1961

This is a favorite stop for lunch of the Road Warriors. The best hot dog anyone could ask for. Three "up"! What I like most, it hasn't changed in 30 years. It's always excellent! My love for Coney Island has been passed on to my children. We will stop any time we're coming through town!

—David Loane, b. 1954

After dance lessons at Cathy Fontaine School of Dance right in downtown every Saturday, I ordered one chili dog and one chocolate milk in a glass bottle. My mother hung out at Coney as a teenager in the 1950s. Her name is in a booth somewhere. This place is a huge part of my childhood memories. I have been bringing my kids here for their entire lives. They are now 17 and 21. Now I live in Milford, but no matter how far, I will always come back.

—Christine Sanderson, b. 1961

I associate Coney Island with family outings. We would come with about 20 people—aunts, uncles, cousins, brothers, sisters, neighborhood kids, mom, dad, and grandma.

—Linda Beaucage, b. 1959

I remember coming to Coney Island when I was eight years old. On a family trip from New York City to Maine, we stopped in Worcester for gas and a bite. When we asked a few locals where to go for lunch, they looked confused, then laughed. Apparently there weren't many places to eat in Worcester back then, but then they sent us to Coney Island. We've been stopping here ever since, including stops on the Greyhound bus!

—Zack Barowski, b. 1968

Coming to Coney Island was always special. My parents came as youngsters and the tradition has continued through them bringing me, and then me bringing my wife and children over the past 51 years. Coney Island itself has not changed. A visit to Coney was always a must when we would return from our travels. Bringing friends and getting their reactions to our favorite Coney Island place always prompted us to say, "It's never changed," and "We love coming here."

—Donat LaRoche, b. 1939

I started coming here with my father in the mid-1970s. As the years passed, I came more often, especially as a teenager. In 1987, I left Worcester for the United States Air Force. This would always be my first stop while home on leave. I got married and had two children. We always come here, year after year. I retired from the Air Force in 2011 and now, when we come from Florida, my wife and two boys insist on coming here as soon as possible. I have passed my love of this wonderful establishment to my boys as it was passed on to me. Hoping it will be here for my grandchildren.

—MSgt Stephen Bachant (retired)

Nous habitons Paris et nous aimons les "chiens chauds." Il n'y a pas de meillieur "chien chaud" que ceux servis au Coney Island. Nous traversons l'Atlantique pour en manger. Woof, woof!

Transl: We live in Paris and we love hot dogs. There is no better hot dog than those served at Coney Island. We cross the Atlantic to eat them. Woof, woof!

—La famille Phillips, Paris, France

I remember coming to Coney Island when . . .

I was 18 years old. Twenty-one years later and I don't think a thing was changed, and I don't think your customers would want you to change anything. Still the fastest, best, cheapest lunch in town. Thank you.

—BOB MAILLOUR, B. 1973

I was 12 years old. Traditions I associate with Coney Island include three "up," a half sour, and cream soda/Apple Snapple." I personally take anyone I know who hasn't been to Coney Island. Special memories I have include eating hot dogs with my Dad, Grandma and sister. I love to leave Coney Island and be reminded of my experience throughout the day.

—BRIANNE JOHNSON, B. 1991

I was five years old. I would come every Saturday with my dad and grandmother. Coming here every Saturday with my family was a special moment of mine.

—KERI TYNEM, B. 1992

I was 16 years old. Wife worked at Northridge Furniture in 1966–1967, came in weekly. I believe the dogs were three for $1 back then.

—WARREN LOHNES, B. 1947

I was 31 years old—LOL! Late bloomers! One day while driving through Worcester we realized that Coney Island was still open. We always thought it was closed down, so we stopped in and both had one hot dog each. We ended up coming back in and ordering two more each. We were addicted! So, every time we come to Worcester, we stop in and grab at least two dogs each. Thanks for having an amazing Coney dog!!

—JEN & BOB

I was 22 years old. I'm a bus driver for Peter Pan Bus Lines. Unfortunately, we moved to Union Station. I miss being able to walk here for lunch. I had to stop as I was headed to Springfield. This is truly the best hot dog establishment. Interested in opening in Springfield? LOL.

—RICKY T., B. 1976

I was 10 years old with my Dad & Mom and seven brothers and sisters. We danced here as teen with our music, our friends. We all loved Coney dogs and chocolate milk, and I do even now at the age of 70.

—REV. RICHARD J.P. CHESNIS, B. 1943

I was nine years old and sitting in the front corner booth with family.

—JAMES VIOLETTA, B. 1944

I was 11 years old. I had not been here before but lots of my family have been. I loved the food. I can't wait to come back and enjoy the yummy food and find my ancestors' names.

—ALEXIA LOUYAKIS, B. 2001

I was eight years old. My dad worked in Boston, so my mom and I would come get him from the bus. I would be in my pajamas eating hot dogs and drinking chocolate milk from the bottle. It was a treat my mom and I shared. Now I enjoy coming here with my kids.

—MARYANNE FONTAINE, B. 1966

I was nine years old. My great-grandfather used to come here, and now every time we come back to Massachusetts, we come and eat at George's. Back home in Riverview, Michigan, there is a Coney Island called "Zorba's," and a picture of George's Coney Island here in Massachusetts is hanging up in there.

—KAYLEE KUBERA, B. 1999

I was seven years old. I brought my cousin. The food is great!

—SAMANTHA DECELL, B. 2005

I was seven years old. The hot dogs were 15 cents then, and I have been coming here for 60 years.

—WILFRED G. BEAUMIER, B. 1945

I was 15 years old. The hot dogs are the same. Everyone came here—awesome.

—DICK, B. 1940

I remember coming to Coney Island when I was 18 years old. We traveled here once a month for your hot dogs and chocolate milk. The hot dogs taste the same, even after 65 years. The décor is the same, too. Now we bring our children and grandchildren. We miss the glass bottles of chocolate milk, which came from Greenwood Dairy. We'll be back soon.

—Gene and JoAnne Giddings, b. 1937

I turned 59 on October 19, 2016. My Dad took me here for my first Coney Island hot dog (mustard only!) when I turned five. I have had hot dogs every birthday since. My father passed away 2/12/2015. His bucket list was down to two things: one more Patriots Superbowl win (check!) and a Coney Island hot dog (mustard only!) which he got the day before he died.

—Terrence (son), William (dad)

I've been coming to Coney Island since the late 60s. My son was only a few years old then and hot dogs were 25 cents or less! Whenever I came in, Cathy, the owner, always gave my son Keith a free bag of chips.

—Russ Gagnon

Climbing over the snowbank to get out of the car, we saw people lining up and watching the parade of people. You were kind to a couple of homeless people and gave them hot dogs.

—Patrick and Linda O'Reilly, b. 1952

When each of our children was born in Worcester, our first stop on our way home from the hospital was always Coney Island. Sorry, but that was the time we carved their names on the wooden booths. Our son Nick is 31. Our son Mitch is 28. Our daughter Jocelyn is 23. They still come to eat their favorite hot dogs and sit in their special booth. Our son Mitch did the same with his two daughters, Trinity and Sage.

—Laura Crompton, b. 1958

I remember my mother, brother, sister, and I walking from downtown during the Blizzard of 1978. I first remember coming to Coney Island when I was four years old. When my son was about eight years old, I took him to Coney Island for the first time with my uncle. My uncle pulled out a buck knife and told my son to carve his name in the booth. My son was so scared, but he did so after my uncle said it was okay. He explained how all the other names got there, and how mine is carved in there somewhere. Then my uncle told him, "One day, you'll bring your kids here to do the same." My son looks for his name every time to this day. He's 14 years old now.

—Keith Duquano

My earliest memory of Coney Island is with my father. We played music on the jukebox, ate hot dogs, and drank root beer from the time I was five years old. We sat in the same booth every visit since 1975. Today, I brought my fiancée in for the first time. We carved our name where my father carved ours 35 years ago.

—Sonja Jasinski, b. 1970

• • • • • • • • • • •

(Left) The jukebox. Photo by Dany Pelletier

I remember coming to Coney Island when I was five years old. It was the place that had the big hot dog sign. Music was always playing and my family danced to it. Maybe the booths did not have quite as many names scratched into them. We were not allowed to do it! The hot dogs and the sauce taste exactly like I remember. I come here now with my children and grandson! The service is fantastic and the people are great! There was no Worcester Center Galleria, no First Night, etc. I grew up in Main South area and we walked downtown to go to the movies (EM Lowes theater, etc.) I live in Auburn now, but I know Worcester like the back of my hand. Coney Island Forever! Thank you!

—Linda Orciuch, b. 1950

I remember coming to Coney Island when I was six years old. Early in the 1960s, with Dad on Saturdays, my three sisters and I would always get chocolate milk. We've been coming here with our children since the 1980s.

—Jeannie Brady, b. 1960

I remember coming to Coney Island when I was seven years old. We always came to Coney Island when one of the six of us made their first Communion.

—Susan Tynan, b. 1956

Two "up."

As a Catholic, we waited until 11:30 pm Friday, then walked from Gardner St. to here so we could have a meal. My parents always sat in the first booth in the bar area. I remember those as the best hot dogs ever, with an orange soda in a glass with a straw.

—Barbara LaPlant, b. 1938

I remember coming to Coney when I was three years old. My parents have been coming in since 1957. My nana, parents, siblings and I always would get the chocolate milk in the glass bottles. We would all sit in the corner booth—all eight of us! I remember my Dad saying, "Where else can you feed a family for under 10 bucks?"

—Anne Russell, b. 1966

I remember coming to Coney Island when I was seven years old. The downtown area has changed so much in the past 10 years alone. My grandfather and I used to come here once a week for many years. He still comes once a week. Being young and having fun with family and friends, I love Coney Island!

—Aimee Berrios, b. 1991

(Left) Two "up" with pickles and chips.
Photos by Rene Burland

I remember coming to Coney Island when I was six years old. I came with my dad. Hot dogs were 10 cents at a the time. Worcester Center was not built at that time. My family and I used to sit behind City Hall where the old bath houses used to be. My dad and I and the members of 243 came after Union meetings every week to eat here and I still do now. Best hot dogs EVER!

—LOUIS KENT, B. 1955

I remember coming to Coney Island when I was six years old. We always had the "dogs" with everything. My dad used to bring in one or two of us kids. Sometimes he would take home a big bag full of hot dogs for a special treat for our large family!

—LINDA JACKSON, B. 1947

I remember coming to Coney Island when I was four years old with my dad, who owned a business on Harding Street, and my uncle Stevie, who grew up down here. Every Saturday, we would come in.

—CHRISTINE M. DULMANY, B. 1968

I remember coming to Coney Island when I was three years old. My dad worked across the street from Allied Trucking. We would have lunch daily and I would read the names on the benches while looking for the names of my parents. I also remember the carnival coming each year across the street. I always wanted to come get a hot dog at Coney Island before we would go on any rides. When I think of Coney Island, I think of my father. This was our special place. I would always ask for quarter after quarter for the jukebox. My father no longer lives around here, but this will always be a special place for our family. I remember looking through a magazine, and guess what I saw? Coney Island as a background in *Maxim* magazine. It's part of a car ad! Don't ever change, unless you decide to open on Tuesdays.

—TIFFANY LEE MILOTTE, B. 1983

I remember coming to Coney Island when I was very small. Coney Island was, and is, a staple for my family on a Sunday afternoon. The place is the same as I remember.

—KASEY KELLY, B. 1954

Coney Q and A

• •

Q. *How many hot dogs do you go through in a day?*
A. A rough estimate would be about a thousand.

Q. *What's the current record for the highest number of hot dogs eaten in one sitting by one person?*
A. Eighteen "up" with cheese.

Q. *Do you have BBQ sauce?*
A. No, sorry. We never carry it.

Q. *Why don't you have sauerkraut anymore?*
A. We never did. You must be thinking of another hot dog stand.

I've told this story many times to my children, grandchildren, and friends. In the mid-1950s as a 13-year-old boy, I would go to Coney Island for hot dogs with their special sauce—even on wintry nights. I would walk home from the Ionic Avenue Boys Club after taking either a woodworking class or playing basketball. Those were fun times, especially if I walked home the long way past Coney Island. I would stop and order two or three hot dogs to go. The combination of smells, warmth, and taste was magical. Passing by Northridge Furniture store, I would check out the window displays while I munched on my hot dog. It was a long walk home, so I tried to take small bites, hoping the hot dogs would last until the Wyman-Gordon underpass. I took my children to Coney Island to enjoy my experiences. Now my children and grandchildren continue the tradition by coming to Worcester and making a trip to Coney Island. Thank goodness I still have the opportunity to taste these wonderful hot dogs. I don't miss the wintry walk home.

—RICHARD A. SHILALE

THE BOYS CLUB

Many of our customers first started coming to Coney Island when they were members of the Boys Club. Originally called the Ionic Ave. Boys Club, the organization is now the Boys and Girls Club and is located on Tainter Street, where it continues its century-old tradition of serving young people.

During the Great Depression, George and Catherine were known for giving out hot dogs to boys who couldn't afford to eat. This generosity created an unbreakable bond between the two establishments. The boys loved my grandmother, and would come in to share their stories about boxing, swimming, watching movies, and woodworking classes.

● ● ● ● ● ● ● ● ● ● ● ● ● ● ● ● ● ● ●

When I was nine years old, we would come to Coney after going to the Ionic Ave. Boys Club. I pooled money with my friends, who were also at the Club, so we could buy as many hot dogs as possible. We would forego drinks so we could buy more hot dogs.

—DONALD COURTNEY, b. 1950

(Above) The Ionic Avenue Boys Club, c. 2000.
From the collections of Worcester Historical Museum

When I was eight years old, I would come down from the Boys Club with my four brothers. I got five hot dogs for $1 at least three times a week.

—RICHARD STARBARD, B. 1952

I used to come from the Boys Club to get dinner. I remember coming here as a kid with my mother and my friends. Now I bring my kids in to keep up the tradition.

—BENJAMIN AVERY, B. 1972

After school in 1967, I would come here with my brothers or friends from the Boys Club. Hot dogs were 25 cents each. Across the street, I remember when the Northridge Furniture store was there that burned to the ground. I was in my teens then. In 1979, I went into the U.S. Coast Guard and, after serving, I got out, got married, had three boys. I take them here even though I now live in Leominster, MA. I had a lot of great times for sure.

—JOHN A. DEMERS, B. 1960

THE PEARLS

Almost fifteen years ago, we Pearls—an eclectic group of women who celebrate friendship and fun—had our first party at Coney Island. Since then we've had over a dozen celebrations on the bar side. Kathy and her Coney Island staff always welcome us with open arms, allowing us to decorate the walls and embracing our silliness (costumes often involved) while we enjoy their hospitality—and dee-licious hot dogs

—LYNN MCCARROLL

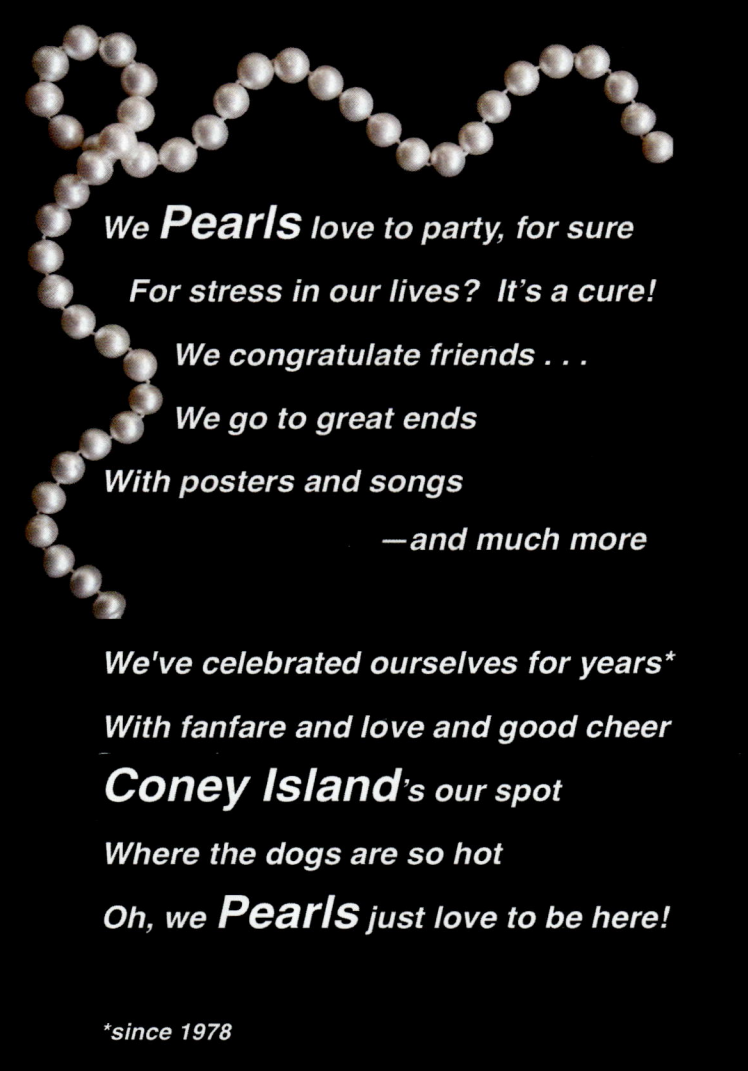

We **Pearls** love to party, for sure

For stress in our lives? It's a cure!

We congratulate friends . . .

We go to great ends

With posters and songs

—and much more

We've celebrated ourselves for years*

With fanfare and love and good cheer

Coney Island's our spot

Where the dogs are so hot

Oh, we **Pearls** just love to be here!

*since 1978

In the late 1930s, my mom and dad came here on every date. They had ten kids, many of whom moved to other states. Whenever my sisters and brothers visited with their families, they would all have to go to Coney Island with my mom and dad. In 1995, my dad was given three months to live. Everyone came to see him. We took Mom and him here. My brother carved a big heart and put Mom's and Dad's names in it: "Rose & Art." I always see Mom and Dad in that booth whenever I'm here.

—SUSAN, DAUGHTER OF ROSE AND ARTHUR RIOUX

When I was four years old, maybe even younger, my parents started taking me to Coney Island. After most Worcester events, like the yearly Wyman-Gordon Christmas party for children of employees, we'd stop in. Rumor has it that my parents met at Coney Island after one of the dances at the Boys Club. Then they went over to Coney to carve into one of the booths, "Ray loves Alice." I've never been able to find it. Thank you for maintaining your integrity and originality of the décor.

—C.R. DOHERTY

(Above) Solon and Joanna Tsandikos, 1970s.

LOVE STORIES

When I first had the idea to write this book, it became apparent that part of it had to be a love story. The love story naturally had to include my grandparents and the many couples who met at Coney Island or had their dates or special celebrations here.

One of the most touching romantic encounters I've ever seen took place here one Valentine's Day. It was the first date for two middle-aged folks who had met a few years earlier. He was over-the-moon smitten. She told us that she couldn't decide what to wear, then settled on a pink top. She handed him a small stuffed animal named "Romeo" as a token to remember the significance of their first date to the tune of a collective "aw" from behind the counter.

Oh, if only these booths could talk, what tales they'd tell! From blind dates to first glances, from first dates to declarations of undying love, from special anniversaries to couples dancing just for fun, Coney Island has always been a special place for love—starting with the original Coney Island love story, George and Catherine, who married in 1933.

I remember coming to Coney Island when I was 16 years old. When I met my first boyfriend, he brought me to Coney Island every day right after the movies. The hot dogs were only 25 cents. We still enjoy Coney Island now, after 60 years of marriage. We have our favorite seat where we carved our names into the booth. And you still have the best coffee around!

—SHIRLEY KACMARCIK, B. 1932

My grandfather was born in 1908, and I recall him talking about bringing my grandmother here before they married. My parents also spoke of coming to Coney Island for date night. I had never been myself until my boyfriend took me here while we were dating. We have now been married 20 years, and still enjoy a great hot dog!

—JENNIFER ALVES, B. 1967

I first came to Coney Island when I was 12 years old. When I was 32, I met a girl, Ann, behind me in line. I asked her to join me for a drink later that night. We got married.

—HANK L., B. 1967

I used to come here with my grandfather, Gerald Shugrue, who was a court officer at the Superior Court. When he took me to work with him, we always came here for lunch. Now I come here with the love of my life, Jamie Harger. The tradition continues!

—SHARON ROBERTSON, B. 1979

One of my fondest memories of coming to Worcester in the late 1960s with my grandfather was coming to Coney Island and listening to the stories of how he would bring my grandmother here when they were dating in the 1920s. Through the years, I have brought friends, nephews, my wife, when we were dating, and now my sons. I hope coming to Coney Island is as special to them as it is to me. I always point out that the chair on display is the chair that was used when my grandparents came here when they they were dating.

—SCOTT SIMOND, SR.

I used to come with my parents beginning when I was 10 years old. Then I came with my boyfriend/fiancé/husband, and now with my children. My husband and I came here many times when we were dating. My husband never knew this place existed until I brought him here. He admired, as my children and I do, that this place always remains the same.

—THERESA AND WILLIAM TOOMBS
B. 1950, 1945

I've been coming to George's Coney Island my whole life. There are four generations of my family in Worcester. My grandparents both met here in the late 1930s. Then my parents met here in the late 1960s. I keep hoping I'll meet someone here, but it hasn't happened yet. Growing up in Worcester, I've seen a lot of businesses come and go, but Coney Island has always been part of my family for many, many years and will continue to be for many more years.

—JOANNA MARCHAND

We have very good memories of Coney Island. My husband and I had our second date at Coney in September 1956. We married 54 years ago yesterday, on July 26, 2012. We brought our three sons and daughter here frequently. We came at Christmas with my children and ten grandchildren to reminisce about the hot dogs and chocolate milk. We will never stop coming. Good memories. Thank you! Merci!

—THE ROGER AND ALINE BOURDEAU FAMILY

We have both come here growing up and when we dated in high school. Every time we come to Worcester for something, we come in for lunch or dinner. We also come every year for Dave's birthday, unless it falls on a Tuesday! We are here tonight because it is our son's 13th birthday and this is where he wanted to come for dinner. We have lots of photos of our family here celebrating. Thank you!

—CHRISTINE AND DAVID DUCHARME, B. 1969

I n this picture, my dad, Reginald D. Hamm, and my mom, Rita St. John Hamm, are "toasting" with Uncle Buddy's wife, Loretta, to left of Dad, and Mom's brother, Leo St. John, on the right. Uncle Leo was a decorated hero with the 82nd Airborne at Battle of the Bulge. Mom and Dad started dating around age 16. She lived on St. John's Road, and he lived on Hitchcock Road in Worcester. His first car was an old, faded yellow, Ford coupe convertible that Mom would have to push to help him start! She graduated from Girls' Trade School. He loved getting together with his buddies at Coes Pond, where they would flex their muscles and impress the girls, but he and Mom only had eyes for each other. Dad, unfortunately, passed in August 1970 at the age of 46. Mom passed in January 2002. She would tell me often that she dreamt he was reaching out to her. My comfort is that I knew they would be together again.

—SHERI WINGERT

Bride and groom (center), Reginald D. Hamm and Rita St. John Hamm. Photo courtesy of Sheri Wingert

W e have been coming here with my dad and mom since I was three. We lived on Green Street and Bartlett Street, which is where Worcester Center is. My dad knew George really well—he used to give out free hot dogs. Now, my husband and I come here on our anniversary for a treat.

—DEBORAH A. FOLEY, B. 1954

When I was 14 or 15 years old, I took the bus from Millbury to Worcester. I would go to the movies. Back then the movie was 10 cents. I would come to Coney Island after, when I was dating my future husband. We've been married 52 years.

—KAREN GAGLIARDI

The first place I drove to after I got my driver's license was Coney Island. When I moved back to Massachusetts after I got married, we came to Coney Island so she could see what I was bragging about.

—BUTCH SAMPLES, B. 1940

Eli and I went to South High together. He was class of '91 and I was '92. We knew each other in passing only. We ran into each other in 1999 and dated long distance (two hours each way) for four years, and committed to blending our families in 2003 in a small town at the halfway mark. Once the children were settled with each other in our new home, we married on November 13, 2004—just after the Red Sox won the World Series! We raised four children together. Two have graduated college, two are in college now, and we are currently raising our nine-year-old, who is conquering the third grade at rapid speed. We've spent 18 years together and it seems like we met yesterday. We are just a simple love story. Every time we visit, we sit at our booth with a heart around our initials: "EMG HG."

—ELI AND HOLLY GILLEN, MADLY IN LOVE SINCE 1999

I remember coming to Coney Island when I was one year old. This place is where it all began. My nana and papa came here on separate dates and left with each other. Ever since then we come as a family and sit in the same area they put their names in the 1950s. I'm a third generation Vallee to come to Coney Island.

—AMBER VALLEE, B. 1996

COLLEGE AND SPORTS STORIES

Worcester is home to more than 36,000 college and university students—even more, if you count the surrounding towns! Every year, we welcome students from Anna Maria, Assumption, Becker, Clark, Holy Cross, UMass Medical School, Worcester State, WPI, and more. Coney Island draws many college and university athletes from those schools for post-game celebrations, as well as serving as a gathering place for kids and families after Little League and Pee-Wee football games, hockey tournaments, or high school athletic events. Whatever the score, hot dogs complete the day.

Kathryn Tsandikos and Harry Kokkinis, President of Table Talk Pies, at a Bravehearts game, 2018.
Courtesy of the *Worcester Telegram & Gazette*

When my son was in medical school, he'd take the bus to New York. I had to run into Coney Island to get hot dogs and chips, only to find that the bus was leaving. I ran after the bus and the driver stopped, saying, "We always stop for Coney Island." He then went back to munching and said, "He was the envy of the bus." As a mom, I was afraid he'd be mortified; but he was proud. In 1968, I remember coming down from Sears, then at 661 Main Street, for lunch.

—RITA SULLIVAN, B. 1946

In 1974, I entered Assumption College as a 17-year-old freshman from Stamford, Connecticut. I did not even know how to spell "Worcester" (Wooster), let alone know where it was. I managed to find Assumption College—or Assumption found me through baseball and a high school teacher who was an alumnus. Soon after landing in Worcester, my friends and I discovered Coney Island. Back then, for one dollar you could get two dogs "loaded." If you had $1.25, you could add a chocolate milk to the hot dogs. The milk came in a small glass bottle. Too many times, I did not have that extra quarter!

I left Worcester in 1976. My family still lives in Stamford. I live in Maine. On my trips to Connecticut, I always stop at Coney Island, usually for three dogs "loaded," a pickle, and a can of Polar Orange Dry. I have two boys who have become fans as well. One is 23 and he lives in New York City, but always has me stop at Coney Island whenever we are passing through Worcester to Route 290 headed to or from Maine.

—KEN PIERCE

I remember coming to Coney Island when I was seven years old. I remember coming here when I would win my minor league and little league games. It was always my main reason to win!

—JASON SLEEPER, B. 1984

I remember coming to Coney Island before the Ice Cats!!

—KRISTEN, B. 1988

My dad went to Holy Cross and told me all about how he and his football buddies used to come here. I went to Holy Cross and my friends and I would walk down when we needed a break. Now my daughter is applying to Holy Cross, and she plans on coming! Three generations of Holy Cross and Coney Island!

—DONNA LAFONTAINE, B. 1959

When going home from Fitchburg State College from 1967 to 1971 by bus, we'd always stop in Worcester before getting a connection to Palmer. We always had to stop at Coney Island Hot Dogs to have the best hot dogs around. I remember watching through the window and seeing the hot dogs being grilled before our eyes. And today, we made it back and the food is as tasty as ever.

—JOHN GOLONKA, B. 1949

(Opposite page) Worcester Bravehearts Opening Day. Courtesy of Worcester Bravehearts

I remember coming to Coney Island when I was 20 or 22 years old. I was a student at Holy Cross from 1982 to 1986, and we loved coming to Coney Island for dogs and beers early on Friday and Saturday evenings, especially after a softball game. We even had our fake awards ceremony at Coney after the season ended. When I returned to Worcester 15 years later in 2001, I was thrilled to see that, despite the many changes in the city, Coney Island was still running strong.

—Ed O'Donnell, b. 1963

I remember coming to Coney Island when I was 17 years old. During college at WPI, I worked at Union Music on Main Street. During that time, my frat brothers from SAE frequented Coney Island for late night snacks after WPI frat parties. We'd sit in a large group in the front corner table and booth.

—Marc C. Trudeau, b. 1961

I remember coming to Coney Island when I was 10 years old. When I would win my softball games or do well in school, my dad and I would come here. It's good to know that the building still stands and has the best dogs. We love this place! Once, my vegetarian daughter decided to try a hot dog and loved it so much, she ordered another one. We introduced my 80-year-old mom to your cuisine for the first time tonight. We came into town today and thought, "Oh, we have to go to that place with really good hot dogs! Unfortunately, we couldn't get our vegetarian to eat one again. It's okay, though. I ate hers! I LOVE CONEY ISLAND!

—Katie McKeon

I always came with my dad as a kid. One of the guys would give us tickets to the Holy Cross football game. When my kids, Jason and Scott, got their licenses, this was the first place they came.

—Dennis Dupre

I have fond memories of my mother's stories at Coney Island Hot Dogs! One story my mother shared with us was that she had to turn over her license to the RMV because she was legally blind. After she stopped in here to eat, she ordered her hot dogs and chocolate milk, but she was a little short on the money. The man who took her order said it was okay and gave her the food anyway. Thank you! My mother was born in 1941 and used to love going to Coney Island. She would order two dogs "up" and two chocolate milks. She passed away in 2009. There is a group of us that comes in here every year on her birthday, June 20, to eat hot dogs and celebrate my mother's birthday, because she would have loved to celebrate her birthday here! Thank you for the memories!

—WENDY NAULT, B. 1973

Some of the stories that have touched us the most deeply are those of people who are now gone but still loved. For instance, there is a man who often comes here and always sits in the same booth, because that's where he used to sit with his Grammy when they came in together. And recently, a young mother came in with her two children for an early dinner. She ordered a beer with her hot dogs and I noticed the children were a little restless.

"Long day?" I asked.

She nodded. "Today is the anniversary of my mom's death," she said. "She loved Coney Island, so I wanted to come here tonight to honor her memory."

Stories of loss are part of the complex tapestry that weaves the many lives together here at Coney Island. What an honor it is to hear these memories. Please read these stories from our customers about the people they have loved and lost. They will bring tears to your eyes, including this one:

Constance "Connie" Skandell Fitzsimmons started working at Coney Island during the Great Depression when she was only a teenager. She was incredibly grateful to have a job when people in Worcester, and around the country, were starving and desperate for money. Connie's grandson, Thomas Rafferty, recalls his nana saying one time she and her family—her parents and eight siblings—had to split an apple because it was all the food they had for two days. While she was working at Coney Island, George and Catherine gave Connie hot dogs to take home and feed her family.

After he returned from World War II, Connie married Francis Fitzsimmons, her husband of 49 years who passed away in 1998. When courting, Connie and Francis came to Coney Island for

Coney Island at night. Photo by Alex Muir

My father was Jack Tubert. A well-known and popular columnist for the *Telegram & Gazette* for 50 years, he made a living out of having his "typing fingers" firmly on the pulse of what made Worcester and its citizens so special. He grew up on the "old" Temple Street, a stone's throw from Kelly Square and a short walk to Coney Island. Throughout his 82 years, eating at Coney Island gave him an inherent pleasure that reminded him of when he was a boy.

Dad often brought my brothers, sisters, and me to Coney Island. Dad would regale us with stories of past glories of camaraderie, favorite booths, and carved initials. As my dad aged, he suffered two horrendous strokes that diminished him physically, but not mentally. It remained a special outing for us to go to Coney Island for a couple of dogs "up" and a longing for a gentler and happier time.

The last time my dad and I were together at Coney Island before he passed away, we were sitting in his favorite booth. I had gotten him his two dogs and a chocolate milk. We were engaged in pleasant conversation about the events of the day. My dad took a bite of one of his dogs. I will never forget that a look of absolute calm came over my dad's face. He looked past me, as if into a reverie of some long ago, middle distance between the past and present. "You know, kid," he said in that hauntingly plaintive voice of a boy who had lived a long and useful life and was now an old man, "They taste like—yesterday."

Tears came to our eyes at the sheer brilliance of what he had just said. The million times we had been together were coming to an end. It's an indelible memory for me. Coney Island is a wonderful bridge for generations of families. Its depth of meaning is so much more than as an eatery. It is an extension of all of our hearts. Thank you for continuing the legacy of beauty.

—Buzz Tubert

dates. As a mom, she brought her three sons and two daughters in for hot dogs and name carving. She even passed along the tradition to her ten grandchildren, which they took to heart.

"I'd call her before I came over for a visit in her last years," Thomas Rafferty said of his nana. "She had the same request every time. She'd say, 'Get a dozen. If you ask for a dozen, it's really a baker's dozen—13!'" Connie liked her dogs "up" and never stopped enjoying the food that fed her and her family through one of our country's most challenging hardships.

In November of 2012, when her grandchildren, Thomas and Joseph Rafferty, sat down to plan her memorial service, Joseph suggested Coney Island. While it has become more common now, in 2012 Coney Island hadn't yet held a memorial service. At first, Thomas wasn't sure Coney Island would oblige and he wasn't sure it was the  right setting. With his brother's urging, he called Coney Island and shared his nana's story. He was delighted to hear an exclamatory, "Of course!"

Connie's family and friends celebrated her life at Coney Island in the bar area. "It was the perfect way to honor my nana," Thomas Rafferty said. "My brother was right."

• • • • • • • • • • • • •

After my dad passed away at the age of 66 in 1971, my mom, after a lengthy period of mourning, asked me to do her a favor. She asked me to take her to Coney Island for lunch like her and my dad used to do frequently. I remember feeling honored by that and "dating" my mom with great pride.

—Jeremiah Adams

Joseph Makowski's 1961 Chrysler.

I grew up in Douglas, as did my dad. Family road trips often were to Worcester and our destination was always Coney Island for some dogs. I graduated from Worcester State, so for lunch or after classes, I'd often head to Coney Island. My Worcester pals also introduced me to Hot Dog Annie's—but that is not in the same league as Coney Island. After I moved to Maine to take a teaching position, my visits home always included a stop at Spag's and, of course, Coney Island. My dad was one of 10 children, brought up on a rural, self-contained farm in Douglas. My dad lived through the Great Depression and also served during WWII. He was a hard worker, but he never went to high school. He worked at the textile mill in Douglas.

My mom did not work, nor drive, so we were dependent upon my father to take us places. My dad kept his cars for a long time. When he ordered the 1961 Chrysler from a small family-run dealership in Uxbridge, he was replacing a 1951 Chrysler. My dad was a mechanic in the service and so he maintained his cars to run for years. There was a lot of self-pride when he took ownership of this beautiful, black car with the big fins. He was proud of that 1961 Chrysler—being so big, it stood out. His friends in Douglas affectionately called him the "mayor of Douglas."

From 1961 'til 1978, that Chrysler was my dad's pride and joy. It took us on many family road trips, again, often to Coney Island. The car sat in his driveway from 1978 to 1999 when it would no longer run. He could not get an inspection sticker for it, but he would not part with it, even though my mom always asked him what he was going to do with it.

Some people wanted to buy it for parts, but my dad couldn't see his car taken apart. When my mom passed in 1998, I asked him if I could have the car so that I could restore it. It was the very first time that my dad ever handed the keys to that car to me. I had the car brought up to Maine and, from 1999 to 2008, the car was slowly brought back to life.

In November 2008, when the photo of the car at Coney Island was taken, I drove the car from Maine and surprised my dad at his house. I told him that I had something to show him. When he saw his baby in the driveway, looking like it did when he first got it in 1961, he got emotional. On the way back to Maine, I stopped at Coney Island, of course. It was not planned, but the last time the car was driven was in 1978, and 30 years later, it was driven once again, and again back to one of its favorite places—Coney Island. My dad, Joseph Makowski, passed away in 2015 at the age of 97.

—JANICE A. MAKOWSKI, SCARBOROUGH, MAINE

My uncle, Paul Corbin, was in hospice care and had one last request. He and my dad, Richard Corbin, have been coming to Coney Island since they were boys, so my uncle's request of the doctor was to allow his family to bring Coney Island hot dogs to the hospital. His request was granted. His daughter came to Coney Island for dogs. He and his family enjoyed another memorable meal together, bringing my uncle's enjoyment for many years. My dad still talks about his Coney Island stories with his brother.

—CHERYL CHICKERING

Coney Island has always been part of my life. Some of my best memories are here. I used to love when I came here with my mother, and she told me about dates with my dad here as teenagers. Every time I feel down and miss my mom, I like to sit, reflect, and enjoy two "up." It's like she is sitting right beside me.

—JILL REYNOLDS, B. 1973

My best memory is loving the chocolate milk in glass bottles with the paper cover and straws, of course— yum! My dad just recently passed away at 83 and, right after his death, my mom, brother, sister, and best friend, who also came with us to Coney Island, came to Coney's for hot dogs. We all talked about how my parents took us here when we were kids and how much we loved it. I love how nothing has changed!

—GINNIE ELIE, B. 1964

In 1989 my mom passed away. This was the last place she wanted to come, too, so I took her here. She was very sick and wouldn't eat before then, but she said, "I want to go to Coney Island to get a hot dog." And she ate it all. She was 72 years old. It is going to be a sad day if Coney Island ever closes. I love it.

—DEBORAH ROY, B. 1959

I grew up in Worcester on Grafton Hill and now live in Acworth, NH, about three hours north. My dad recently passed away, and one of my fondest memories is him taking the two boys here to eat in his 1951 Chevy pickup when he worked for Bancroft Motors. I remember standing at the counter and ordering from a man with a gray mustache. The hot dogs were 35 cents and milk was served in glass jugs. Now I come here whenever I am in town. Every holiday I come and get six with everything as a Christmas present for a friend up North.

—CARL BABBITT

Growing up in South Worcester near Sacred Heart, I recall great memories of my family. There were four kids at the time, walking to Coney Island many times. My mom died of breast cancer when we were young. We still all come and think of the great memories we shared in those seats! Just driving by puts a smile on my face.

—PATRICIA COLLINS, B. 1961

Photo by Dany Pelletier

Part 5
CONEY ISLAND INSPIRATION

I took this photo (above) at a time when I had been planning to move away from Worcester and wanted to bring along pictures of all the places I hold sacred. Coney Island has had a special place in my heart since I was a kid, and my dad would take me after picking me up from school on Vernon Hill. These days I bring my stepdaughter, whenever we're in the city, to get our two "up" with mango Snapple. She affectionately calls it "the hot dog place with stories in the drinks." George's has been a treasure in this city for the last 100 years and holds a lot of happy memories. I hope it will be here for at least 100 more. It's truly an honor to be included in this celebration.

—CASEY WESTERLIND, @CASEYWILLSHOOTYOU

Coney Island has inspired people of all ages to create art in every form you can imagine. From poems to tattoos, from Instagram photos to illustrations and paintings, this art has helped introduce people around the world to the magic of Coney Island.

New York Times best-selling author/illustrator Jarrett J. Krosoczka creates books with humor, heart, and a deep respect for his young readers. The illustration above is from *Hey Kiddo*, a graphic memoir about growing up in a family grappling with addiction, and finding the art that helps you survive.
Courtesy of Jarrett J. Krosoczka and Writer's House

I grew up in the Grafton Hill area loving our Saturday treat back in the 60s and 70s. Going to Coney Island was such a great memory and still is! I remember watching the hot dogs up the arm and patiently waiting as we ordered hot dogs with my chocolate milk. Life was good!

—MARK TONELLI, @TONELLIDESIGN

(Opposite page) Photo by Mark Tonelli

CONEY ISLAND ARTISTS

Step into Coney Island today, and at first glance, it might feel like a time capsule. There are the same booths, etched with names and initials. Here is the same bar and tiled floor. Yet, glance around at our customers, and it's clear that the next generation has embraced us. There might be a guy on his phone, checking his email while he waits to order, or a couple of friends taking selfies in one of the back booths, while a woman reads a book on her Kindle. We're happy to say that the next generation seems to love Coney Island as much as their parents and grandparents did.

An image from *American Squares* by Leah Frances, The book is based on an Instagram
project that documents American cultural relics and iconography. See also p. 40.

I simply saw the sign ... actually, it was only the storefront of George's, somewhere online and always wanted to see it in person. My husband and I planned a trip around my birthday, November of 2016, and stayed overnight in Worcester. We drove that night to see the place but it was closed and raining, torrential rain! The next day we went back and were allowed in before they opened. It was truly a gorgeous place, obviously full of history. I hope I can go back, with sunnier skies and a wide angle lens! (Photos opposite page and p.40.)

—LEAH FRANCES, @AMERICANSQUARES

I am a Worcester native and have been coming to Coney Island for as far back as I can remember. I've always loved eating here, and can honestly say I have never had anything but hot dogs from the menu. I always order them the same way: three "up" with a bag of chips. I started simple when I was a kid, one dog and a drink. I was hooked from that point on.

Friends and I have met here over the years from high school, college, to dates before movies (no onions for those nights). Now, as an adult, my love for Coney Island has evolved into my career as an artist. That love had to be expressed through my sculpting. The iconic neon sign and wonderful building have been burned into my mind. I had to create a piece. When it's done, it will be made into a bank for, what else, hot dog money! I sculpted the piece out of wax and will make small plastic banks from the original sculpture.

My hope is people will buy a bank (right) and save all their change to come to Coney Island, so they can share experiences and a few laughs with their friends and family over delicious hot dogs, just like I have done for so many years. Thank you, George's Coney Island, for always filling my stomach with great food and my mind with wonderful memories.

—MIKE ACKERMAN,
THE ECCENTRIC EASEL

Coin bank
by The Eccentric Easel

Coffee mugs by Mugged in Worcester

I moved to Worcester in 2007 and have had a Coney dog at least once every other month. I grew up in Pittsfield and ate at the legendary Teo's Hotdogs as a kid. It was awesome finding a nostalgic and unique experience like George's here in Worcester. When I lived in Marlboro in my twenties, I would make the drive to Coney every once in a while. I started Mugged in Worcester in 2014, and when I was thinking of places to include, Coney was near the top of my list of iconic places. I was able to create a decal from a photograph in order to apply it to my handmade mugs. I used the slip-cast method of making mugs from commercially made plaster molds and sold them on Etsy and locally at Crompton Collective and Worcester Wares.

—JONATHAN HANSEN, @ MUGGEDINWORCESTER

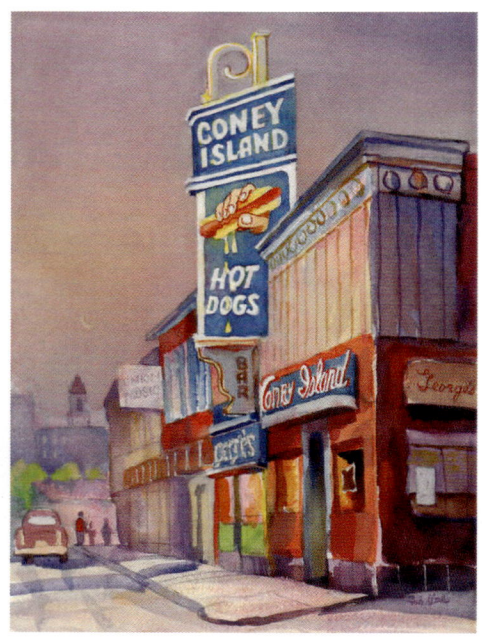

Known for his stylized renditions of regional diners, roadside attractions, and pastoral scenes, "Diner" Don Sawyer's watercolors may be viewed at selective arts and craft shows and purchased at numerous fine gift shops. "Diner" Don commented, "Most rewarding on my 'road art' journey have been the folks I've met along the way." WWW.DONSAWYERART.COM

Always a fun place to go. Years ago, an art gallery owner told me I should do a painting of Coney Island. This is one of the latest ones.

—ROBERT N. AIELLO, B. 1944

Coney Island is a Worcester institution. I've been a patron since I was a kid. I believe my grandfather brought me for my first time. He owned a machine shop on Franklin Street and would eat at Coney Island regularly. I'm weird: I like mine with cheese, ketchup, chocolate milk, and sour cream and onion chips. I'm a telecom engineer by day, photographer by night. I like surreal imagines and colorful, detailed photos. Once I started in photography, I knew that sign would be a subject for me.

—BOB BERNIER, BOBBERNIER.COM

(Above) Watercolors by Don Sawyer and Bob Aiello

(Left) Photo by Bob Bernier

114

I've lived in Massachusetts my whole life. I grew up just west of Worcester in Warren, and am now currently living in Marlborough. I'm a photographer and have recently been getting more involved in the flourishing art community of Worcester, and I am loving it! Worcester is a fantastic city full of so many inspiring individuals.

Every year, my family has had a tradition of taking my grandfather to Coney Island for his birthday. He was a bit of a stickler on where he wanted to eat, and we found Coney Island was the only place he really loved to go. He lived out in Shutesbury—so it was always a trip to take him out to Worcester.

We always sat in the same booth: the window seat to the right of the door as you walk in. Our names have all been carved into the booth and over the years have become increasingly hard to find amidst the masses. It was no challenge for us to order upwards of 15 to 20 hot dogs for the family, always the works. We'd pick a song on the jukebox, and make sure to grab some chocolate milk and pickles. My grandfather passed away in 2009, but we've continued our tradition and still go for his birthday every year. It's still considered one of the family events, so I always try to take some photos when we go. Coney Island will always be close to my heart!

—ALLISON SEPANEK, ALLISONSEPANEK.COM

(Above) Photo by Allison Sepanek

I was born and raised in Millbury. One of my most enduring memories is going to Coney Island with my grandfather. We'd always just sit and talk, get two "up," a root beer and a bag of chips. Years later, I began to take my kids there. We'd sit, talk, and eat. I can't drive by the place without feeling good. The fact that so little has changed there in my lifetimes makes it all the more special. As I walk in, the memories are that much fresher.

So what does this have to do with my pictures? The short answer is I shoot things I like. I shoot things I think look cool. I like color. As you can see, depending on when you shoot the sign, the colors can change completely. Day time looks different than late afternoon, than night, etc. That makes it fun. The hard part is that when I started shooting seriously, I knew the sign had been shot a million times from every angle. What could I do to add something different? Aside from the phone edits, which I did waiting for my son to get out of guitar lessons next

door, I decided to sort of deconstruct it. I knew taking shots of parts of the sign would tell the story, as anyone around here knows it. I zoomed out with the shutter open. I picked up my camera and shook it. It's sort of a challenge. In a nutshell, I picked Coney as a subject because I can do what I love, at a place that I love, surrounded by memories of people I love, then eat the best dogs on earth. If there's a heaven, it can't get much better than this.

I've been taking pictures seriously since 2012. I like to have fun. I want my pictures to be fun. To me, photography isn't always about getting the perfect shot. It's about going out and having a good time. It's about learning something new, seeing things from a different perspective, and trying to capture a moment in time that I want to remember. I live in Worcester with my wife Julie, sons Alec and Bradyn, and our dog Molly.

—ALEX BELISLE, BELISLEIMAGES.COM

Photos by Alex Belisle (See also p. 134)

I am from Worcester County, born and raised. I have been coming to Coney Island since I was a child. I took this photo (left) when I was taking a photography course at Framingham State University. I was experimenting with night photography. I have many artistic interests and styles, and I have explored and experimented in many different genres and media. My interests and experiences range from writing poetry, essays, and journals to drawing and painting, photography, animation, and web design.

—MICHAEL J. WEST, MICHAELJWESTDESIGNS.COM

(Left and on cover) Photos by Michael J. West.

I'm a 36-year-old local photographer who grew up in Paxton but spent most of my time in Worcester. I have lived all around the city in various apartments and love to show people the ins and outs that they don't usually get to see. I'm a self-taught photographer who loves working with color, and I feel like my photos are meant to be printed large.

—JAMES KUSZ, @JAMESKUSZPHOTOGRAPHY

(Below) Photo by James Kusz

117

We love when local photographer, Mike Henderickson, uses his skills to capture Coney (right). He makes us look good. To marvel at more of his work see also pages 1, 44, and 70, or visit:
UNITYMIKE.COM or NEXTDAYWEDDINGS.COM.

Mark Waitkus gathers inspiration for his art from historic stadiums, legendary teams, and memorable moments in life. His expressive brush strokes and use of color bring his watercolors to life, providing a feeling of being a part of the nostalgia he recreates. His work has earned accolades with numerous clients including Major League Baseball, the Boston Red Sox, St. Louis Cardinals, Detroit Tigers, Cal Ripken Jr., Tony Gwynn, Gaylord Perry, the Cooperstown Baseball Hall of Fame, The New England Sports Museum, and The Jimmy Fund. See below, and also pages 2 and 11, or visit:
WAITKUSSTUDIOS.MYSHOPIFY.COM.

My grandfather and father were born and raised in Worcester. My great-grandfather was the Rice in Tucker & Rice Plumbing Company. I grew up visiting, and we always, always went to George's at least once each time we were there. My dad remembers eating 13 "up" at once on a dare. (They were a nickel or dime, I think, when he was a kid in the 1940s.)

I remember getting take out and eating in the parking lot of Benson's Animal Farm when I was a kid. I've passed down the "stop at George's" tradition to my kids. Any time any of us are driving through, we stop to grab a couple to eat in or take out, often to a family reunion where our order might top out around 40 (and still we can be in and out of there in under 15 minutes!). I've yet to sit on the bar side and have a beer. Someday! My favorite order is two "up." Then one "up" to go.

I take photos of/at George's every time I'm there. Whether it's to send a photo via text to family and incite their jealousy or to post to Instagram, I always want to memorialize my stop. I almost always take photos of the exterior and of the stoop, too.

—LYNN RICE SCOZZAFAVA, @LYNNANNERICE

(Above) Photo by Lynn Rice Scozzafava

INSTAGRAM ART

After receiving Lynn's photo and story (left), we asked her to interview her father W. Donald "Don" Rice, a retired pilot now living in Pine, Colorado. Don, born in Worcester, Massachusetts in 1933, was kind enough to oblige.

Lynn: What is your first memory of George's Coney Island?

Don: My first real memory is having George's picked up and brought home, usually by my dad. My first solo trip I was around 15 years old with a 16-year-old pal, who had his license. From the time I was 15 until I left Worcester at 21, we'd go with a car full (or two) of friends, at all hours. Whether for lunch or after the movies, we'd be there. And if we didn't go ourselves, we'd send a friend to pick up a box and bring it to wherever we were. My record in one sitting was eight. My earliest recollection of how much a hot dog cost is 15 cents. My father, W. Maynard Rice (1909–1992) grew up eating George's and remembered when they were 5 cents.

Lynn: What do you remember about Worcester growing up?

Don: I remember everything. At eight years old I got a "yard pass" and never looked back. I had a voucher for the trolley and rode it from one end of the city to the other, north to south and east to west.

I was a YMCA kid, and it was a short walk from Shepard Street to the Y at 766 Main Street. I spent hours there and at Y camps. In the winter after swimming, I'd walk home with frozen hair. The YMCA saved my life and prepared me for the Air Force. I went to Classical High School. My mother had gone to Commerce and my father to North. I went to WPI but decided the Air Force was a better fit for me.

Lynn: What's your favorite Coney Island order?

Don: Five "up" and a cold beer. It's not just quality; it's quantity! Always "no onions."

I am a lifelong Worcesterite and have been going to Coney since I was very little. My earliest memories of Coney Island would be of my dad taking me for a hot dog and a chocolate milk after the movies. He still gets a chocolate milk with his hot dog … he's 83! The photo was taken June 29, 2017. My hubby and I stopped in for lunch. Couldn't resist a lemon pie! Everything on the table reminded me of the flavors I grew up with.

—GINA TEMBENIS, @TIPPYTINA

I have a long-standing connection with Coney going back almost 20 years to when my dad brought me for the first time. Over the years I have gone almost monthly, and then even when I moved away from Massachusetts, we would make a visit each time I came home. I took this photo the first time I came back to the establishment after moving back to Massachusetts. I enjoy adding the cartoon-style to the image.

—JOSH BIERNACKI, @JBIERNACKI77

I'm a lifelong Worcester girl, so Coney Island has always been in my periphery. As a teenager I scratched my name along with forgotten crushes into the seats along the rear left wall. It's a place that evokes the yesteryear nostalgia of my grandparents' and great-grandparents' Worcester. It is a must-stop for any out-of-town visitors and it is always a hit. Although I no longer eat hot dogs (sorry), I have been known to imbibe a beverage or tackle a bowl of chili in recent years. My husband, on the other hand, usually orders three "up." It's a place we love returning to again and again for the pure authenticity of Worcester, the atmosphere and the memories.

—JENNIFER O'LEARY
5TH-GENERATION WORCESTER GIRL, @BLUESTDOGGY

I love the colorful mural on the back of Coney because this area of Worcester always looks grey to me. Of course, the Pow Wow Worcester mural campaign brought much more color to the area. I still feel the yellows, orange, and red on this building give off such a warmth. The other (top right) is of the iconic sign, which needs no intro!

—KEITH GREENE, @KEITHGREENE

This photo (below) was taken in November 2015. A friend and I made a stop in on our way home from NYC. My obsession with George's Coney Island started long before that. It began in the mid-1990s while I was a student at UMass. When driving home, we'd often hop off the Pike for a dog. Well, it was never just one! Now, whenever I pass by or through Worcester, a visit to George's is mandatory.

—BETH BRESNAHAN, @BETHBRES13

I've been going to Coney Island since I was a little kid. My father used to own a paint store right next door to the building. Lunch at Coney Island was my form of payment for working with my pops for the day! I keep it classic on my order: three dogs with onions, mustard, and relish, Wachusett chips, and a Polar seltzer. I took this photo when I was visiting back home. I lived in Denver at the time. Going to Coney Island was the perfect cure for my homesickness!

—DAN FOLEY, @DANIELMURTAGH

I grew up in Millbury, so I've been to Worcester and Coney Island many times. I worked right down the street from Coney Island at the *Telegram & Gazette* for a summer. I took this photo (left) while having lunch with my parents and sister. She had just earned her master's degree from Worcester State, and I thought treating the family to Coney Island was the perfect way to celebrate. I'm no expert photographer, but I love documenting great food I'm eating, especially when it's at a local favorite.

—Neal J. Riley, @realdealneal

I have lived in Sutton for about 20 years. I am a private chef and baker. I previously owned a gourmet shop in Grafton. I grew up in Sudbury. In the mid-1960s, my grandfather and I stopped at Coney Island on the way to his hometown in Williamsport, Pennsylvania. That was the start of my love of Coney Island hot dogs! Fifty years later, I still take my children for the always-delicious chili dogs (below) with cheese and lots of onions!! We have always appreciated that it will always be the same! Consistency is key to a successful business, and Coney Island has nailed it for 100 years!!!! Food to me is love!

—Renee Burland Nilo
@renee _ burland _ nilo

Call us the game-shakers. IgWorcesterMA is the unofficial brand of Worcester, Massachusetts. We take on the role of breathing new, positive life into the city, which was once known for its innovations and inventions. Throughout history, Worcester led New England in the fields of technology and entrepreneurship, and we want to make sure no one forgets that. With a distinct focus on revealing the secrets that make Worcester great, we highlight local businesses, entrepreneurs, city architecture, events, and amazing local leaders through a series of workshops, pop-ups, and collaborations. Our mission is to bring back the vibrancy that once boosted city pride among Worcester residents. Our mission is to show how beautiful Worcester truly is, all while highlighting its potential to be better. We want to help make the city shine! Tag us or use #igworcesterma to be featured on our social media outlets.

—Jaime Flores Photography
@jaimefloresphotography

I've been a Worcester kid my entire life, born and raised. I've been going to Coney ever since I was a little baby. I still have my name carved in a booth somewhere. My favorite order is two "up" with cheese, a pickle and a Narragansett draft. When I took the photo, I hadn't been in for a few months. One day, I just decided to drop in when one of my old friends was in town. When I got my order, I thought it was gorgeous, so I had to snap a picture and post it.

—Dan Tobojka, @dantobojka

I grew up in Worcester and often visited the restaurant. My uncle worked there as a teenager. My favorite order is actually the cheeseburger with ketchup and onion. I took this picture when my husband delivered the *Telegram & Gazette* in the area. I often rode in the car and took pictures of various Worcester sites.

—Bonnie De Silva Porfirio, @bonnie _ gabrielle

I moved to Massachusetts from North Carolina in early 2016, and started working in and around the Worcester area. I've always been interested in history, vintage things, and good food, so when my boyfriend—he is from the area—said there was an iconic place he wanted to take me, I was all in. George's Coney Island has been a go-to for me ever since! My favorite order, 3 dogs all the way and a cream soda, was the first order I ever tried. On colder days, I HAVE to add in a side of mac & cheese!

My very first visit there, I probably stood out as a tourist inspecting the place and snapping shots of just about everything. I really wanted to document the feel of George's Coney Island, and to convey the sense of history that is there, from the curved shape of the order counter and the lights, the name-carved booths, the original Coney Island chair, the vintage tiled floor at the entrance (above), and of course, the infamous neon sign! Every time I come back, I notice something different and it gets added to the series.

I have always been creative in one fashion or another, whether it's photography, visual art, or restoring furniture. I have been creating art and other pieces for your home (basically a little bit of everything!) with my small online businesss, NerdyGirl Design. Our newest venture is Outside the Box, an Escape Room business in Webster, Mass.

—Jennifer Harrington, @jiffner777

George's Coney Island is my favorite place ever!
This picture I took a while back. Looking at it is
making me hungry now.

—EJ O'ROURKE, @EJOROURKE41

My family is from Connecticut and my sister
and I grew up eating your hot dogs. I have
lots of fond memories and Coney is still my favorite
after 35 years. My Dad and sister discovered Coney
by accident one day when we were very young. They
took my mother and me soon after, and we have
been going back ever since.

—TEKLA MOQUIN

I'm a Worcester native who has loved Coney Island
Hot Dogs since I was a kid. My favorite order is
two "up" with a birch beer. I always take dates
there to see if they can hang. I may have carved my
name in a booth a million years ago in high school.

—PENELOPE E. ANGIULOL
@PENELOCOPTER

TATTOOS

It was the fall of 1998 and AOL chats were all the rage. I met a wonderful woman who I needed to meet in person. Chats turned to phone calls, then came bus trips. The Peter Pan bus arrived in Worcester around 11 am. Shannon was waiting there for me. She said there was a good place to eat nearby, so we walked around the corner. When I first saw the magnificent signage, I was in awe. When I walked in and had the full George's Coney Island experience, it was magical. The smiling faces and friendly folks behind the counter made me feel so welcome. Four months later, I took one last bus trip to Worcester. This time it was a one-way ticket.

Shannon and I are married and have two children. I lived and worked in the city for the next ten years. Working for Sheldon's Harley-Davidson, we would all come down together. Nothing is more Worcester than George's Coney Island. I already had many other tattoos, but I had been saving this entire forearm for the magical place that welcomed me to Worcester.

—JUSTIN EWELL

Justin Ewell's forearm tattoo by Justin A. Buduo (photo inset) of Studio 31 Tattoos and Fine Art.

I grew up here in Worcester. My grandfather used to take me and my brother, Chris, here once a week. Chris and I would always get three dogs, "just sauce." My Gramps would get a ketchup, mustard, and onion. We would always sit in the third booth up the middle. I'm sure you would be able to see our family name carved into the bench.

After our Gramps passed, we continued the tradition, especially now that we both have families of our own. We'll bring our kids and enjoy some great Coney dogs. Yes, I still order three dogs with just sauce, but I also order one with ketchup, mustard, and onion in remembrance of our Gramps. I'm pretty sure that my brother does the exact same thing.

I'm an internationally known and award-winning artist based out of Studio 31 Tattoos and Fine Art, located at 436 Park Avenue in beautiful Worcester. I've been tattooing for more than 18 years now. I am well-versed in many styles of tattooing, but I focus mainly on color realism—portraits, floral pieces, and animals. I'm always looking to push my art to the next level, so I strive to make each piece better than the last. When I was asked to do this piece, I was beyond excited. Seeing that George's Coney Island has been a part of my life growing up, and continues to be a part of my life, to do this tattoo, I felt like it was an honor.

—JUSTIN A. BUDUO, TATTOOSTUDIOS31.COM

Zaza Ink is family-owned and has been in business in West Boylston since 2001. Joe has been tattooing for over twenty years, specializing in realism and portraiture. Joe and his amazing group of tattoo artists stand by their work and their professional opinion to not let you leave with a future regret.

Five generations of the Brooks family have dined at George's Coney Island. Before moving away from Worcester, Shane wanted to take a piece of home with him. "Wherever I am, I've got something to remind me of where I'm from. Nothing says Worcester like George's Coney Island," Shane said.

(Right) Shane Brooks' tattoo by Joe "Zaza" Peterson (photo inset) of ZaZa Ink.

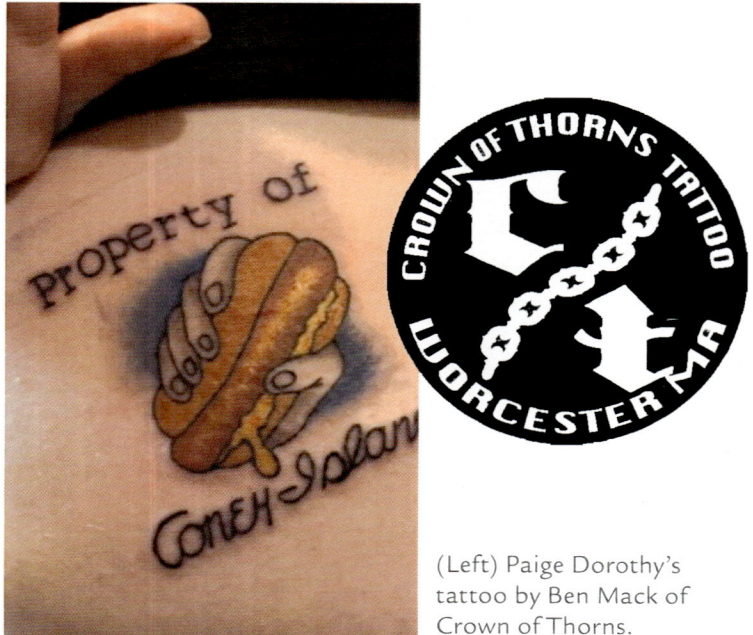

(Left) Paige Dorothy's tattoo by Ben Mack of Crown of Thorns.

The mission of Crown of Thorns, located at the base of Grafton Hill in Worcester, is to create an environment of creativity, friendship and tattooing that is "clean, classy, and bold as tattooing is intended."

I'm from Worcester and I grew up going to Coney Island with my grandparents. Out of all the hot dogs I've had in all my travels George's Coney Island is still my favorite. My inspiration for this tattoo was a few too many White Russians at brunch. The artist who made this was Ben Mack, Crown of Thorns.

—PAIGE DOROTHY

HOT DOG!
A STAND UP SIDESHOW

HOSTED BY
SHAUN CONNOLLY

CONEY ISLAND
158 SOUTHBRIDGE ST · WORCESTER MASSACHUSETTS
2ND THURSDAY OF THE MONTH
8 O'CLOCK PM

The idea of the show at Coney Island came first. The history, the carvings, the people and, of course, the hot dogs seemed like the perfect backdrop for some additional character. I just didn't know what the show was going to be. So I thought of the actual Coney Island in Brooklyn, and I thought of its amusement parks and all of the characters crawling around the boardwalk. I thought about a game wheel and the other challenges that can be played while at the beach enjoying a dog. Then I thought about the buzz and excitement of Worcester's Coney Island, I thought about the comfort of the place, the warmth of the grille, and the aproned workers. It felt like kismet.

I know this show is mine, so I'm biased, but it is an absolute hoot. Everyone who performs raves to me about how great the show is, how fun the crowd is and how wonderful the staff is. I guess that last sentence sums it up; all of that is why we have this show at George's Coney Island Hot Dogs, where else could it be?

—SHAUN CONNOLLY

COMEDY

One of the changes at Coney Island has been a push from staying open late to closing early to focus on the larger lunch crowds. However, it may not always be this way. We've added events to bring energy into the restaurant.

Worcester comedian Shaun Connolly had been organizing comedy shows for six years when he approached us with an idea for *Hot Dog! A Stand Up Sideshow* in 2014. Up to ten comics a night come from all over the country and spin the Coney Island Wheel on the second Thursday of every month. The Coney Island Wheel dictates what kind of set the comic will do. The Coney Island boardwalk in Brooklyn inspired Shaun's idea to have a game wheel for each show.

Shaun Connolly, a comedian born and bred in Worcester, has produced and performed in comedy shows for more than ten years, and hosted *Hot Dog! A Stand Up Sideshow* at Coney Island for three of those years. He also has hosted a monthly talk show, *The Sort of Late Show*.

Local artists Ryan Gardell and Kai Griffiths painted an 80-by-30-foot mural as part of Pow! Wow! Worcester, a ten-day citywide initiative where 32 artists created 29 murals throughout the city.
Photo by Spencer Shea, 2017

Q: *What made you think of Coney Island for the Pow Wow mural project?*

A: The POW! WOW! team saw Coney Island as a significant institution in the downtown area and wanted to find a way to engage the historic and beautiful building/signage with contemporary street art. Looking at the booths inside Coney Island, as well as Kathy's openness to adding to the legacy of the building, it was a perfect fit, and who better to paint than two Worcester artists that grew up on Coney Island Hot Dogs.

—Che Anderson, Deputy Cultural Development Officer, City of Worcester and creator of Pow! Wow! Worcester

Former Governor Deval Patrick with Kathryn and staff.

PUBLIC FIGURES ON CONEY

Tim Murray introduced me to George's Coney Island when we were campaigning. What a treasure! Great dogs, affordable, no fuss, friendly. Even my troopers perked up when we made a swing by. And I could always count on a good dose of good-natured political teasing with my order. Congratulations to Kathy and the whole Tsandikos family on 100 years of great service.

—FORMER GOVERNOR DEVAL PATRICK

George's Coney Island is truly an iconic landmark in Worcester. I am humbled by the legacy left by George and Catherine Tsagarelis and honored that their granddaughter, Kathryn Tsandikos, has chosen to carry on their traditions in our great city! It is extraordinary for a family-owned business to sustain and adapt to the many physical and cultural changes that occur from one decade to the next. George's Coney Island has been, and continues to be, one of Worcester's most beloved destinations for locals and visitors alike.

—EDWARD M. AUGUSTUS, JR., CITY MANAGER

Over its 100-year history, George's Coney Island Hot Dogs has become, not simply a place to order one of its famous hot dogs or a hamburger, it has also become a central gathering place for people from Worcester and Central Massachusetts. People from all walks of life come to Coney Island with their family, friends, or co-workers to share a moment and an affordable family meal that is unique and memorable.

It is a place where grandparents bring their grandkids to share stories about how their own grandparents once brought them to this same place, and had a hot dog in the same booth where they are sitting. It is the same place where a governor of Massachusetts can enjoy a hot dog with his daughter—as Deval Patrick did—while sitting alongside a neighborhood dad with his daughter, both enjoying a laugh about the carvings on the booths, while washing down a hot dog or two with a Polar soda or chocolate milk. It is a place where all are welcome—judges and janitors, truck drivers and teachers, doctors and dishwashers. It is a place welcoming for teenagers on their first date or an elderly couple reminiscing about times gone by.

It is an unspoken refuge that provides a moment to remind us that, while time may not stand still, we can enjoy a bit of the past and maybe walk out the door with a new memory that will last a lifetime. It is a place that makes Worcester and all who visit feel special.

—TIMOTHY P. MURRAY, PRESIDENT & CEO
WORCESTER REGIONAL CHAMBER OF COMMERCE

Two Up and a Bag of Chips

In 1996, Worcester artists John LaPrade and Christine Murphy-Cross mounted an exhibition at Coney Island entitled *Two Up and A Bag of Chips*. 1,848 hot dogs were hung from the ceiling and inspired the curator of The Evelyn Sharp Collection at the Guggenheim Museum in New York to write this letter (left) to the *Worcester Telegram & Gazette*.

By using this Coney "trademark" ordering phrase as the title of their exhibit, John and Chris also inspired the title of this book almost 25 years later!

Social media doesn't just show us photos. It also allows us to get to know our customers. We love to post questions and wage healthy debates about Coney-centric topics like …

What's the best beverage for this meal ?

Shawn FitzMaurice: High Life.

Kathy Mae: Chocolate milk or a 'Gansett.

Mike Bastek: 'Gansett.

Steve Tayor: Cold beer.

Steven Cook: Polar seltzer and chips (sour cream and onion).

Judy Mrozinski Hoenig: Chocolate milk.

Chet Witkowski: Another hot dog and chocolate milk in a bottle …

Tommy Boutiette: Chocolate milk.

Greg Asadoorian: What goes best with a couple hot dogs? About three more hot dogs!! And chocolate milk …

Virginia Johnson-Sears: Moxie.

Aaron Smith: Grape soda.

Katelyn Sarah Kiefer: Polar root beer all the way!

Mike Shannon: Birch beer is the only way to go.

Katie Palatucci: Moxie!

Joey Gomez: Snapple Apple.

Casey Thebodo: A chocolate milk, a bag of sour cream and onion chips, and a sliced deli pickle.

Justin Levins: Three with sauce, a bag of Wachusett chips and a grape soda!!

James Broadard: Wormtown Be Hoppy

Linda Marcus: Chocolate milk, that the old dudes would flip the paper tops off of with an ice pick.

Susan Niddrie: I'm old school—chocolate milk is the way to go!!

Leana Marie Desantis: Chocolate milk hands down!!!!

John Wypyszinski: I was taught by my father and grandfather that the ONLY thing that you drink with your dogs is chocolate milk, which I've passed on to my kids. Got to teach 'em right.

Teri McHugh: My grandparents, my parents and then my brother and I always had chocolate milk with our Coney dogs!

Keith Gajewski: Moxie!

Suzanne Gula LaPointe: Water, I don't want to take away from the Coney Island dog with anything. Favorite place to eat hot dogs.

Gene Jones: When I was a kid, 55 years ago, it was a chocolate milk in a glass bottle with a paper cap on the mouth. The counter help would pierce it with an ice pick AND you would drink it through a paper straw that you wouldn't want to bite down on because then, you wouldn't be able to sip through it. That was BP … before plastic.

Brittany Schold Gasco: My 18-month-old thought chocolate milk. I'm partial to a nice ginger ale.

Liz MacGregor Blanton: Chocolate milk! There's no other way to have Coney Island!!!

Christine Hurley: Has to be chocolate milk. Our Gram introduced us to Coney happy memories.

William Peter Pisaruk: Come on, Chief. You need a Sam Lager!!!

Pattie King-Oberg: Grew up having chocolate milk with my everything hot dogs from Coney Island Worcester. The best …

Linda Medeiros Pellerin: Polar cream soda!!

Marie McKeon: Miller High Life!

Tim Clark: Always root beer with hot dogs.

Dennis Carboni: MOXIE!

Frank Pettengill: Cream Soda

Genie Wassel: Final Answer—CHOCOLATE MILK!!!!!

Doc Siddall: As a child? Chocolate milk. Adult at lunch? Polar Beverages Ginger Ale. Adult at dinner? Bottle of beer.

Bob Zukowski: Always three with two chocolate milks, for about 59 years.

(Above) Al Toney enjoys a beverage with his lunch at Coney Island. Photos on this page and opposite by Dany Pelletier

What is your hope for Coney in the next 100 years?

Paul Provencher: To continue as a true Worcester success story, and not to change a thing … Keep that deep-rooted nostalgia the same as if it were new.

Janice Makowski: Totally agree.

Karen Donahue Welch: Ditto.

Ruth A. Hathaway: I always look forward to my Coney Island hot dogs when I come home to visit. I try to go at least two or three times while there. I'm 78 now and remember going there when I was about five. Not only nostalgic, but great hot dogs.

Marie Remillard Barry: Don't change. Keep your old NEW you, please …

Bill Sinclair: Another 100 years.

Robin Gardner: Please don't change. My childhood memories are filled with trips to Coney Island with my dad. I joined the military in 1976 and moved away to Alaska, but I returned just last year to see family and, of course, came by. I felt embraced when I came in the door by all that was so good back then.

I just couldn't stop grinning—everything was the same. Please don't change.

William Eaton: Don't change a thing. Keep it cash only. Don't change the George's side either.

Erica Fairbanks-Bemis: In the coming years, I would love if Coney would offer sauerkraut, pretty please? I think Worcester will be unrecognizable—but in a good way, so much going on.

Paul Dumas: Let it be the same in 100 years.

Steven Boudreau: If I have a choice, I want my last meal to be four "up" with BBQ chips and a chocolate milk. And I hope that is in 100 years.

Martin Kolodziejczak: My hope is that Coney Island never changes.

Stephanie Hunter: Don't change a thing! Keep that grape Polar stocked!

David Zonia: Very fond childhood memories. Always went there after church on Sunday. Didn't have much money in the early '50s. It might have well been the Waldorf Astoria.

Part 6
A LOOK TO THE FUTURE

George's Coney Island Hot Dogs celebrated its 100th Anniversary on September 30, 2018 with a festive block party.

We were playing on a music tour and friends said, "You have to go to Coney Island hot dogs. It's an American institution." Can't imagine why Bruce Springsteen or John Cougar hasn't put you to song. All the best from the Canucks (that's Canada).

—Roy Johnstone and Steve Sharratt, PEI

I am from Mars. On Mars we have no hot dogs. Whenever I am in the Worcester area I zoom in for a hot dog at Coney Island.

—Gurg D. Martian, PHD (professor of hot dogs)

(Opposite page, see also p. 116) Photo by Alex Belisle
(Above) Solon Kelleher, George's great-grandson, at the 100th anniversary party.
Photo by Habbakuk Media Service

Coney Island Is KNOWN FOR HOT DOGS

Dear Coney Island,
Thank you for having us today. I know that Coney Island was founded in 1918. My experience was great because the hot dogs were amazing. 5 star review. Nice service.

Sincerely, Jyce from Nativity School Worcester

Coney Island's 100th anniversary celebration. Photos by Habbakuk Media Services

george's CONEY ISLAND Est. 1918
CONEY ISLAND CELEBRATING 100 Years
HOT DOGS

My husband grew up in Worcester. I came from Millbury. We both grew up with George's Coney Island and maybe crossed paths there through the years. It wasn't until after we were married that I overheard my husband tell a friend he married me because this is my favorite place for hot dogs. The only place. May you be here another 100 years!

—Jody & Bob Jerscyk

To me, Coney Island is not just a place to go get a couple of the best hot dogs, but a place I can go and remember all the good times with my grandfather, and the many new memories with my wife and kids.

—Andrew Ianniccheri

CELEBRATING 100 YEARS

A few years ago, a woman asked if she and "The Pearls"—the group of women who gathered regularly to celebrate milestones like anniversaries and birthdays (see p. 97)—could hold a retirement party at Coney Island for one of her friends.

"We'll need lots of red wine," she added.

Of course I said yes. Now The Pearls gather here whenever they have a special occasion to celebrate, sometimes bringing 80 people to gather in our booths and listen to the jukebox. This is how lifelong friendships and memories are made, and Coney Island is the perfect place for that to happen.

(Above) Shaunalee Reyes and Raymond Portalatin enjoy hot dogs "up." Photo by Dany Pelletier

137

Serving customers with a smile.
Photo by Dany Pelletier

TELEGRAM & GAZETTE | telegram.com | Friday, March 23, 2018

George's Coney Island timeline

1918 A luncheonette is established on Southbridge Street that would eventually become George's Coney Island. The woman who ran the luncheonette had the recipe that would become Coney Island's "secret" chili sauce.

1929 George J. Tsagarelis, a Greek Immigrant, opens George's Coney Island.

1933 George and Catherine A. (Angelopoulos) Tsagarelis get married and run George's Coney Island together for many years.

1938 Wooden booths are added in the dining room, marking the last major change done on the premises.

◀ **1940** Russian immigrant S.C. Romanoff designs a 40-foot-high neon sign, featuring a gigantic hand holding a humongous hot dog in a bulbous bun, which is bolted to the building façade. George Tsagarelis is the uncredited hand model for the iconic sign.

1955 Rev. Solon S. Tsandikos, a Greek Orthodox priest, marries Joanna A. Tsagarelis (George's daughter). He would eventually help run George's Coney Island for many years.

1980 George Tsagarelis dies. His wife, Catherine Tsagarelis, continues to run the business with the help of her son-in-law, Rev. Solon Tsandikos, for many more years.

2000 Catherine Tsagarelis dies.

2018 Kathryn T. Tsandikos, the daughter of Rev. Solon Tsandikos and granddaughter of George Tsagarelis, runs George's Coney Island.

Are George and Catherine looking down on these and other special moments with smiles on their faces? I feel certain they must be, for they built Coney Island with their own hard work. They must be as proud as I am—if a little bit stunned—to see the important place this iconic restaurant holds today, not only in our lives and in the lives of our customers, but in Worcester's history.

Today, this unique city is still welcoming immigrants, just as it did in my grandfather's day. These newcomers are working hard to open new businesses and restaurants with the flavors of Jamaica, Ghana, Latin America, and the Middle East, adding to the mosaic of English, Greek, Irish, Italian, Polish, and other cultural traditions already established here. We're thrilled to still be on the scene after a hundred years, watching as this great city keeps reinventing itself.

Writing this book has taught me so much about the place I call home. Sharing the memories of my family, along with the memories of many of the people who have experienced Coney Island through the decades, is my way of not only paying homage to tradition, but of expressing my excitement about the future. I can't wait to see what's next.

POEM, 1960

She took me
to Coney Island Palace,
a Worcester icon.
Beat up booths.
Graffiti walls.
Broken tile floors
Hot dogs to die for.
Treated me to chocolate milk,
a 10-year-old's fantasy.
Out at night, sibling-free,
undivided attention.
In her weathered apartment,
we make a puzzle, eat almond candies,
another first.
My Polish auntie godmother tells me
Stories, over-excited I fall asleep.

—SHARON A HARMON

Fourth-grade paper, 1989

MY LIFE AS A DOOR KNOB

I kind of like being a door knob, but sometimes it's a
drag. People are always touching me and kids touch
me with greasy hands as they are leaving. But, most
of the time, I like being one.

—IRENE PALEOLOGOS

At Coney Island there's always a customer or two
Some day that customer may be you.
For the hot dogs people come to eat
They have gift certificates for you to treat.
At Coney Island there are hot dogs galore!
Every week they get boxes more.

—ALEXIS KELLEHER
GEORGE AND CATHERINE'S GREAT-GRANDDAUGHTER

George and Catherine's great-granddaughter, Alexis Kelleher, wrote this poem while growing up at George's Coney
Island helping her mother, Kathy Tsandikos. Alexis' son, Reed George, was born in November 2019.
He hasn't started serving customers yet.

Kathy Tsandikos at Coney's 100th Anniversary celebration.
Photo by Habbakuk Media Services

Acknowledgments

Looking back on the process of writing this book, it's hard for me to believe that nearly seven years have passed since I first considered the idea of creating a history of my family's restaurant. "Packrat" isn't a word you'd want associated with a family restaurant, but my family has undeniably accumulated countless boxes of articles, photos, and records, now spanning more than a century. I was looking through stacks of boxes one day, when I realized that these artifacts tell a narrative that is dear to me and maybe to others as well. I had a vision of what this story could mean to the people of Worcester and beyond, but the task at hand was insurmountable for me to achieve alone.

I've spent the last few decades of my life running George's Coney Island, raising my children, and caring for my aging parents. Writing a book, on the other hand, is not something I've had much experience with. I realized that I needed help to realize the vision of this book.

Tom Hostage, of Bespoke History, was the first collaborator who offered to listen to my ideas. His assistance was invaluable in getting this project off the ground. Without him, I surely never would have brought the initial stage of this book into existence. Tom was persistent in helping to organize my thoughts even as my life interfered with the project. I can't thank Tom and his team enough, including his daughter, for their patience, initiative, and belief in this project.

Lauren Muscarella and Holly Robinson were invaluable in the writing of this book. Lauren expanded an outreach program to gather stories from our beloved customers and fans. Holly helped put my thoughts and ideas into words. She is owed a debt of gratitude for her many visits to Worcester and her guidance. Through our work on the book, she and I have become dear friends. When I was going through moments of self-doubt regarding this project, Holly saved the book from death at the drawing board on more than one occasion.

I needed a publisher, designer, and editor for the book, and into this role stepped Worcester native, Ingrid Mach of TidePool Press. She has become a friend, and I owe her thanks for moving the project along to its conclusion. She and her colleagues, Rob Zeleniak and Linda Chadwick, were able to translate my vision for this book into a finished product with precision and imagination.

While the professionals above certainly helped in the process of making this book, none of Coney Island's successes would be possible without our beloved customers and fans. Many became contributors and shared their stories and memories. They made this book a community effort, and my heart is full of gratitude to them. I thank our customers for their generosity and willingness to share their stories with us, and you, the reader.

Lastly, I want to thank my family and staff for their support and patience while I worked on this book. It has been a journey. Each of the following has played an important role: Harry Kokkinis, Alexis Kelleher, Solon Kelleher, Laura Porter, my mother, Joanna, who passed away before the completion of the book, and my father, Solon, who many of you knew as Father Solon. I am grateful for their support, patience, encouragement, and love.

Now is the time for you to enjoy the fruits of our labors. I hope that in reading this book, you gain a sense of appreciation for the people of Worcester, the roles of local restaurants in a community, and, of course, hot dogs.

Coney Island staff, 2020:
(Left to right) Xiomara Olivencia, Megan McCraw, Brendan Vargeletis, Buki Paloja, Eric John Yankus Franco, Solon Kelleher.

And one more thing . . .

In the time it has taken to complete this book, the world did a radical 180-degree turn. In March 2020, due to the COVID-19 pandemic, George's Coney Island closed for indoor dining for the first time.

The staff drew together as a family and continued to serve our customers with enthusiasm and love. To them and to you, our loyal customers who support us, I say a huge and heartfelt THANK YOU.

Testimonial Index